Victorian Lady on the Texas Frontier

VICTORIAN LADY ON THE TEXAS FRONTIER

The Journal of Ann Raney Coleman

EDITED BY

C. Richard King

UNIVERSITY OF OKLAHOMA PRESS
NORMAN AND LONDON

FRONTISPIECE: Ann Raney Coleman
(*courtesy Duke University Library*)

International Standard Book Number: 0-8061-1980-2

Library of Congress Catalog Card Number: 69-16721

Acknowledgments

Editing a journal such as Ann Raney Coleman's is not a lonely task, nor is it the job of one individual. For those many persons who have contributed, in one way or another, to this project, the editor feels a keen debt.

Especially does he wish to express appreciation to his mother, Alice Neill King, for taking notes, making appointments, and checking facts; to his sister, Mrs. B. J. Arnall, for making trips to the Houston Public Library and the Brazoria County courthouse in pursuit of information; to Mrs. L. G. Rich, who called the journal to his attention, chased elusive names through Daughters of the Republic materials, and made available the original manuscripts and documents in her private collection of Republic of Texas papers.

To Miss Kathleen Blow, chief reference librarian of The University of Texas, who has a magical way of locating information; Mrs. Virginia Gray, assistant curator of the Manuscript Department of the Duke University Library, who was courteous and efficient in making the original journal and letters available for study.

To Ronald Seeliger and his staff of the Newspaper Collection of The University of Texas; to James Day and members of the staff of the Texas State Archives.

To friends and associates who have patiently listened to problems and progress reports without grimacing.

To many members of the faculty of the Department of Journalism of The University of Texas who met the editor's classes, enabling him to consult the original journal.

To these and others who have contributed, the editor expresses appreciation.

C. RICHARD KING

"Doughoregan"
Stephenville, Texas

Introduction

The Author

On March 31, 1882, Ann Raney Coleman, then seventy-two years of age, wrote an attorney in Austin, Texas, about her attempt to convince the state legislature, through her representative, that she was due an allowance from the state of Texas "to aid in my support, and get me a small home." The lawyer, James B. Goff, appealed to Governor O. M. Roberts that following his investigation of the case he was "satisfied . . . that her statements are true and that she is as deserving if not more so of some bounty from the state as many who have received Veteran Certificates." Mentioning that "she is very old, bears an excellent character and is very needy," Goff suggested that a "donation of a small piece of the public domain which the Railroads hav'nt gobbled up" would be "well-timed charity."

When the veterans of the Battle of San Jacinto held a meeting in the Opera House in Dallas on April 20, 1886, to mark the fiftieth anniversary of the battle, Ann Raney Coleman presented a petition, asking them to help persuade the legislature that she deserved a pension.[1] She

[1] *Dallas Morning News*, April 21, 1886.

explained the trip to Dallas to her niece in this manner: "Had a free ticket to go and come and then my expenses on the road was twelve dollars which has left me without any money."[2]

The trip to Dallas and the resulting endorsement by the veterans of San Jacinto did not bring the desired results to Mrs. Coleman, however.

Who was Ann Raney Coleman? What qualified her, as late as 1886, to petition for a bounty of land from the state of Texas?

Born in Whitehaven, England, on November 5, 1810, "a strong and healthy" baby, Ann Raney became "so fat and strong that the gayest clothes and prettiest bonnets failed to improve" her. Her earliest recollections were of her "father's country seat, a pleasant spot" with a stream "so clear we could see the bottom of it." Ann, her brothers, John and George, and her sister Mary enjoyed fishing for trout and bass, playing on the rich lawn, and riding Herring, the Shetland pony for which their father had traded a barrel of fish.

Ann's mother, "kind, gentle, amicable . . . energetic in her housekeeping . . . proud to her superiors, but to those in humble life, most gracious," was the daughter of a rich merchant of Whitehaven. As a bride, she brought "three thousand pounds on the day of her marriage," but John Raney, "in pursuit of a wife and not a fortune," could only rejoice in his choice on both counts.

[2] Ann Raney Coleman to Alice Smith, May 1, 1886, Manuscript Division, Duke University Library.

Ann's father was "a fine looking man with good complexion; fine hazel eyes, very soft; high forehead; five foot eleven inches in height." He was serious, sober, and grave, and upon the death of his father, he found himself "possessed of fifty thousand pounds Sterling, and four estates." He took his father's place as partner in a bank.

When bankruptcy charges were filed against John Raney, Ann, her brothers, and her sister were taken by an aunt and uncle, who proposed to send the children to school in the neighborhood. "The school," Ann wrote later, "was situated on a high hill near a castle about one thousand years old," and the castle proved to be a favorite resort during recess.[3] The walls, once eight feet thick, were in a decayed state, but the flowers struggling from the crevices were "sweet, very sweet." One day, while walking among the vines, Ann found a gold ring and a Queen Anne coin. The school, however, was a disappointment. Ann had little respect for her teacher, a man thirty years of age, "surly and cross in disposition," and given to self-esteem. She decided that she "was as good a scholar as my teacher, who appointed me to hear lessons, saying I had quite as much learning as was necessary and would keep me in practice."

Later, it was decided that Ann and her mother would open "a first class boarding house" in Liverpool, and three

[3] The castle around which Ann Raney played was built by Henry II, son of William the Conqueror, some time between 1172 and 1177 and is regarded as one of the finest examples of Norman stronghold remaining in England. Fragments of its walls and its principal entrance, Black Gate, and the southern postern remain. It was this castle which gave the town of Newcastle its name.

days after boarding the schooner *Triton*,[4] they began preparations for the new endeavor. The mother was busy "laying in new furniture, beds, and bed clothes, [and] all kinds of kitchen utensils," while Ann superintended the arrangement of furniture. John Raney joined his family in Liverpool to go into business for himself.

Ann's brother John, trained as a gunsmith, went to America where, six months after arriving, "he breathed his last sigh in a small log cabin on Oyster Creek[5] not many miles from the Brazos River in Texas, on Mr. Warren Hall's place."[6] As Ann wrote in her journal, "Mr. and Mrs. Hall were kind to him in his last months, filling the last sad task which a parent, so far distant, could not do so."

The father left Cumberland, England, for Texas in 1829, after filing brankruptcy proceedings. In Texas, he

[4] Shipping notes appearing in the London *Times* at this time indicate that the *Triton* was a British schooner making regular runs across the channel.

[5] Oyster Creek, which rises north of Richmond in Fort Bend County, Texas, flows southeast fifty-two miles through Brazoria County and empties into the Gulf of Mexico. Some authorities believe that Cabeza de Vaca first set foot at the mouth of Oyster Creek. Later colonists, under Stephen F. Austin, developed large plantations along the creek, which was banked with rich alluvial soils. Walter Prescott Webb (ed.), *The Handbook of Texas*, II, 321–22.

[6] Warren D. C. Hall was listed in an advertisement in the *Telegraph and Texas Register*, September 23, 1837, as living at East Prairie. That year he was owner of China Grove Plantation, located approximately eight miles above the old town of Anchor. An advertisement in the *Telegraph and Texas Register*, March 14, 1837, gave his home as Brazoria; he was offering for sale, at auction, the land and stock from the plantation of Benjamin F. Smith, "lying and being east of Oyster Creek."

became a teacher for the Brit Bailey family in Austin's colony. That he was acquainted with Stephen F. Austin is definite, for the empresario mentions John Raney in his papers dated November 23, 1830.[7]

Using a "thousand pounds out of annuity" which had been set up by a bachelor brother, Ann's mother made arrangements to join her husband in Texas. Ann recalled:

We were one month getting ready to go to America. Each day was spent at the stores or dressmakers. Then came the packing of each trunk; every day brought its work until we were off. My oldest brother's vessel arrived before we left, only in time to say adieu. He wished me to remain in England, saying he would never let me want for anything. But my uncle B would not listen to him, saying that my going was indispensable. That my mother was getting up in years and that my sister was too young to take care of her.

On February 1, 1832, the family left Whitehaven for Liverpool to board the *St. George*, a merchant ship laden with ballast but no cargo and destined for New Orleans. Ann's uncle had, through the captain, made arrangements for the Raneys to have "every comfort" during the passage.

Ann waved farewell to Henry Marks, her beau, who "had a disposition like a mule; he could be led, but not drove; warm and faithful in his affections, jealous as Othello." As a parting gift, Henry presented Ann with a ring "and his picture in water colors on ivory, which

[7] Eugene Barker, *Annual Report of the American Historical Association for the Year 1922*, II, 539.

next to my brother's, I kept with care during the '36 war with Mexico. In traveling one night I lost the ring."

On February 14, 1832, Ann, her mother, and her sister set sail.

After the death of both parents in Texas, Ann married John Thomas in what she called "the first public wedding in Brazoria." Her sister Mary married Samuel Hoit. After the death of her first husband, Mary became the bride of Dr. Benjamin Harrison, one of the mysterious men of early Texas.

In her appeal to Governor Roberts, Ann commented that she and her husband "lost all that we possessed, in the Strugel [*sic*] for Independence and did never recover from our losses, so that when my husband died in '47, I found myself homeless with one child to educate." In the same letter she recalled that "at the Battle of Velasco I moulded bullets and made the patches, and took them on my horse 15 miles, to Mr. Bertrands ranch for our men to come after them. I was persued by two spies, but had the best horse, and made my excape[*sic*]."

John Thomas was not a participant in the Battle of San Jacinto because "he had his arm broken by the fall of a tree and could not make an efficient soldier." He did, however, send a substitute to Fannin's army at Goliad. "At the breaking out of the war he was appointed a home guard to see the wiman and children safe to the Sabine line along with maney other disabled Vetrens. He was at the battle of Velasco and maney other smaller battels [*sic*]."

Like many of their neighbors and friends, when word

reached the scattered river-bottom settlements of Texas that Sam Houston and his troops were retreating, the Thomases joined in the "Runaway Scrape," leaving Texas for the safety of the United States.

When they reached Donaldsonville, Louisiana, Ann and John settled on the plantation of Charles Henry Dickinson, who had come to Bayou Grosse Tete, seventeen miles west of Baton Rouge, at the insistence of his grandfather Joseph Erwin and had opened Live Oaks Plantation. When the Thomases arrived, Dickinson, in his thirties, was one of the most landed owners of fertile acres in the "garden spot of Louisiana," but a man whose background had been saddened when his father duelled Andrew Jackson.

The Thomases later purchased their own plantation, and the Pointe Coupee Parish census of 1840 listed John Thomas as head of a household including two males under 5, one male aged 40 to 50, one female under 5, and two females between 30 and 40. He possessed fifteen slaves, six of whom were engaged in agriculture. His slave holdings included two males under 10, seven between 10 and 24, one between 36 and 100, three females 24 to 36, and two females 36 to 55. His family consisted of his sons Edmond, born in Texas, and George, and the daughter, Victoria.

Ann continued to have close ties with Texas. In the summer of 1852, she wrote the tax collector of Brazoria County for information about the league of land that her father had received December 16, 1831. She learned that the land had been redeemed by "Charls Burkly," whom she had employed to pay taxes for the years 1850–52. In August she wrote the comptroller of Texas to determine the taxes due on the land, which was located in Matagorda County on the west bank of the Colorado River. Again, in September, she corresponded with the comptroller, declaring that Burkly had purchased the half of the property belonging to her sister; she inquired about the amount of taxes due on her half. If the place had been sold for taxes, she continued, "let me know what steps to take to redeem it."

Life in Louisiana was tragic for Ann. Her two sons and her husband were buried in Louisiana soil, and her second marriage, to John Coleman, proved hasty and unfortunate.

In June, 1854, Ann Coleman left Louisiana and boarded the steamer *Baltic* in New York to check on her family estate in England and to visit old friends and relatives. She returned to the United States on the *Baltic* in August. The *New York Times* welcomed the 195 passengers on board the *Baltic* with a story on the front page of the August 21 edition. Ann's trip to Texas was delayed by the low water in the Mississippi. "The air is parched, the streets are dusty, and the mid-day heat is intense— although every morning and nights are cool. No rain of consequence has fallen here for nearly seven weeks."[8] On Saturday, August 26, however, there was great excitement brought by a thunderstorm. "The earth drank in the wel-

[8] *New York Daily Times*, August 23, 1853.

come flood with eager joy," wrote a reporter for the *New York Daily Times*. "Corn-stalks rustled their satisfaction and potatoes rolled in their moistened beds with intense delight. The rain was reasonably heavy and fell steadily until midnight."[9]

Ann returned to Texas, sued John Coleman for a divorce in 1855, and saw her daughter married and separated from Dr. Joseph Waldrop. Once again finding herself in the center of action, Ann was living in Lavaca and Matagorda when Federal troops stormed the Texas coast during the Civil War. By teaching in public and private schools and by doing household work, Ann Raney Coleman struggled for a livelihood after the war, moving frequently, quarreling often, and fretting occasionally over the lack of attention on her daughter's part, but finding solace in prayer and in quiet walks through the woods.

The Journal

From her temporary home on Garcitas River, Victoria County, Texas, on March 17, 1875, Ann wrote her niece in North Carolina:

You say you would like to have the history of my life. I do not get time, my child, to write it for you, as it will be a big book when compleated but I wish to get it Published some day. Then you will have it. My own family have never read it. I have kept it very secret, as I do not want its contents revealed, untill it is Published.

[9] *Ibid.*, August 26, 1853.

The aunt reported progress on her reminiscences, promising May 3, 1876, "you will be sure to have it some day." Thirteen years passed, and the promised manuscript remained undelivered; on March 25, 1889, Mrs. Coleman reassured Alice Smith, "I will not have the work on my Book done before the last of April, so you will be [*sic*] time enough to pay the express for it. I am working every day hard to copy it so I can send you one copy."

Finally, on October 14, 1889, she rejoiced, "My Book is ready for you, when you are ready." On a more somber note she added, "I thank you for the Paper and Stamp, as I find a difficulty to get either haveing no way of makeing money. . . ." Her financial depression did not lessen, for on March 25, 1890, she wrote, "I do not have the money to pay the expenses on it [the book]. I aught [*sic*] not to have taken the three dollars you sent me for my own use as I know you need every dollar yourself."

In her reminiscences, copied on one side of the sheets of seven notebooks, then stitched together with twine, Ann often used initials rather than names, but in letters to her niece, many of which fortunately have been preserved, she referred to the individuals by name, often narrating the same incidents in both journal and correspondence. Her letters frequently were written in violet ink, the paper then turned, and crisscrossing lines penned over those already written. Although hopeful throughout much of her life that someday she would receive income from her parents' estate in England, she confessed to being "as poor as a church mouse,"[10] and this confession probably explains her need for conserving paper.

Ann Raney Coleman had qualifications for writing a book other than having lived a life she considered "as variable as the colors of the rainbow." Throughout the voyage from England to America, she kept a journal she sent to Henry Marks, her fiancé, soon after her arrival in New Orleans. While living at Port Bolivar, on Galveston Bay, in the spring of 1873, Ann wrote in her notes complaining about her failure to hear from Mrs. Clara Stanton:

She is indebted to me for forty dollars, independent of the Book which I wrote for her, for publication. I wrote her three Books, and was to have half, as soon as she sold them. She is now living with her Sister at Corpis Christa [*sic*]. Her sister is keeping a boarding house. I leave her in the hands of God, trusting that one day her conscience will haunt her.[11]

Her reminiscences, laboriously copied in final form for her niece (page 116 has been removed from the notebook), and her letters are voluminous, so Ann obviously enjoyed writing, often letting her dreams drain through her pen onto the paper to be preserved for the future, using the writing to fill lonely hours and mentally bridge the vacant caverns in her heart.

The journal ended when she learned that her only

[10] Ann Raney Coleman to Alice Smith, September 24, 1877, Manuscript Collection, Duke University Library.

[11] Ann Raney Coleman to "Dear Eugina," March 30, 1873, *ibid.*

daughter was doomed with cancer. The daughter, Victoria Watson, died August 10, 1890, and Ann became ill the same day. For three weeks she remained under a physician's care,[12] and a letter edged in black and addressed to "my dear Cousin" was sent by Addie Saldana on March 25, 1891, stating, "Our grandma is not so well. She has a very bad cold and has not been so well, poor old lady. She is failing in health every day. She will not live long, I am afraid."

But Ann Raney Coleman bounced back, writing her niece in the fall that she needed to raise thirty-six dollars to supplement the nine-dollar monthly pension the county allowed her.

The Manuscript

In a letter to Mrs. E. L. Lehman of Angleton, Texas, dated July 3, 1947, Dr. Samuel E. Asbury, late faculty member of Texas Agricultural and Mechanical College, explained that the Ann Raney Coleman journal

fell in my lap from a blue sky. Miss Nannie M. Tilley sent it to me from Duke University Library, Durham, North Carolina. When I first saw the Manuscript, that was the first I ever knew of Ann Raney. Miss Tilley wanted me to evaluate it. Well, I translated Ann into good English . . . and sent around the first three books. We all decided it was the greatest find in Texas history for years. When Miss Tilley heard that, she was crazy to get it back, of course. But I prevailed on her to let

[12] Ann Raney Coleman to Alice Smith, October 15, 1890, *ibid.*

me complete the translation of the seven "books." Later she made me three laborious verbatim typed copies. . . .[13]

To Miss Harriet Smither, Texas state archivist, Dr. Asbury wrote in 1946, "You fear that the Ann Raney documents are not important, but they are very important. The dates are important and the addresses of Ann are particularly important."[14] Miss Tilley wrote Dr. Asbury on June 22, 1944:

I am somewhat inclined to believe that the bulk of the manuscript should be published with some minor omissions. It seems to me that even her own religious effusions should be published. You have observed no doubt that her religious outbursts came at times when she had little to do. Some of it isn't bad. She showed signs of thought.[15]

The niece for whom the journal was prepared, Alice Smith, was married to E. V. Melchor and lived in Mooresville, North Carolina, until her death in 1908. No children survived.[16] The Ann Raney Coleman manuscripts, purchased in October, 1941, from Mrs. C. E. Mills, Mooresville, by the Flowers Collection of the Manuscript Department of Duke University Library, contain the journal, three letters written by J. Locke Smith to his brothers, two undated letters by Mrs. Mary Raney Smith, and

[13] Collection of Mrs. L. G. Rich, Stephenville, Texas.
[14] Dr. Samuel E. Asbury to Harriet Smither, January 16, 1946, Asbury Papers, Texas State Library Archives.
[15] Nannie M. Tilley to Dr. Samuel E. Asbury, June 22, 1944, Asbury Papers, University of Texas Archives, Austin, Texas.
[16] *Ibid.*

personal letters from Ann Raney Coleman to her niece. A typescript copy of the journal is in the Archives Department of the Texas State Library, Austin.

This Edition

To facilitate reading ease, the editor has corrected Ann's spelling of general words, leaving intact her charming spelling of proper names, a spelling which indicates that she relied upon pronunciation. Because the author of these reminiscences punctuated by a jerk of the pen rather than by well-defined commas, periods, or semicolons, the editor has taken the liberty of supplying punctuation marks for the convenience of the reader. Additional paragraphs have also been marked, and the chapters, "books," as Ann Raney Coleman termed them, have been redivided. Mrs. Coleman divided her story into seven notebooks, paying no attention to the change in subject matter. The entire Book 1, Ann's early life in England, has been dropped from this volume, and severe editing has been applied to other divisions. Sections removed by the editor are shown by increased spacing or ellipsis between paragraphs or by ellipsis within paragraphs, and the editor's additions or condensations of lengthy material are placed within brackets or in paragraphs of italic type.

Contents

Victorian Lady on the Texas Frontier

Second Book

Letters had been coming from my father for six months urging us to join him with all possible speed. We were now going to that father I loved so much and who loved me in return. . . . Night approached and we were in the English Channel on *St. George*,[1] where we remained ten days, blowing gale after gale until every seaman was perfectly exhausted with labor. The cabin was often full of water, and for several days at a time we had not a dry thread upon us. Had this state of affairs lasted a day or two longer, I think some of us must have died, for we were sick from the cold we suffered and the want of fire and comforts we could not have, owing to the roughness of the weather.

Our captain was a rough, unpolished man, had but little sympathy for females, drank to excess, lived most of his time in bed, and never came on deck but to give

[1] The *New Orleans Bee* of April 16, 1832, notes that the brig *St. George*, which left Liverpool on February 16, had been towed by the steamer *Shark*, Howren, captain, to the New Orleans port. The *Bee* of May 30, 1832, again listed the brig among the ships clearing the port and indicated that the vessel belonged to B. Booth & Co.

wrong directions to the man at the helm, whip the seamen, and insult us females; and although we paid him 60 pounds for our passage, he deprived us of every comfort he could, seldom if ever giving us a good dinner unless I went and cooked it myself. He was provided with everything good to eat, but was such a brute that he did everything in his power to make us feel our dependence upon him. He was hated by both passengers and crew, although there were only two steerage passengers besides ourselves. And it was only when he was a good deal intoxicated, then I stole his keys and got what little comforts were allowed us by the owners of the ship. Captain Garret himself was part owner of the *St. George.* The keys hung in his state room on a nail, and he did not think anyone would presume to take advantage of him, whilst he slept, to get them. In this he was mistaken. I not only stole his keys, but went to the little house where they cooked and prepared enough dainties to last several days, the cook assisting me to dispatch my business in as much haste as possible, whilst I, with the stealth of a cat, went and hung up the keys.

At twelve o'clock in the day the captain and the mate would take an observation of the sun and make their reckoning. They always differed about the distance we had come; the mate was right, the captain wrong. We had been about eight weeks on our voyage when one night about sunset, I saw the mate look very serious. I told my mother. When she asked him the cause, he replied that we must be close to some of the West India Islands, and he was afraid we might run upon some of them in the night. Owing to the dissipatedness of our captain, we had run out of our course. If the captain had kept his right reckoning we ought not to have come near them. My mother and self begged him to keep a good lookout, which he did, sitting up that night himself and kept watch. He was a sober man and a good seaman.

About four o'clock in the morning, the mate ran down into the cabin and called the captain to get up and come on deck quick. "We are on an island." The captain did not take time to dress, but jumped out of bed quick. "What is that?" cried the mate, "Is not that an island, speak?" But he met with no response. The captain was frightened. The truth was plain. The mate took the helm and carried the vessel softly across the rocks and course until day broke. A sight presented to our view, a danger no one could look upon without a shudder, a barren rock upon which we could have thrown an apple loomed up before us. Not a sprig of grass or shrub grew upon it. It was called the Island of Neves.[2] We sent up a prayer of grateful thanks to that Being who has said the hairs of your head are all numbered; He who cares for a sparrow, how much more for us! Our lives were spared by the temperance of the mate who never drank. God had willed it so. What a fate would have been ours had we been wrecked upon those rocks! No pen can state the thankfulness of every heart on board that ship. The vessel was steered safely by our mate,

[2] Probably the Island of Nevis, a fifty-square-mile island of the Leeward group in the British West Indies.

out the breakers running mountains high, the roar of which might be heard many miles away. They sounded like a death dirge; the sea gulls made a pitiful noise as though they said you have escaped a fearful end. When day broke we went on our way rejoicing.

I spent my time pleasantly on board the *St. George*, sometimes fishing, reading, or writing to my friends in England. I kept a journal of our voyage to pass away the time, which, on our arrival in New Orleans, I sent to Henry. I sometimes mended stockings for the second mate, Mr. Cotton, who was the son of a rich merchant in Liverpool and chose a seafaring life in preference to any other trade. He was a gentleman in manners and appearance, not handsome but good looking, graceful and easy in his deportment, and refined and of no small literary attainments; a sunburnt complexion, fair hair, hazel eyes, tall and well formed. He was bound, as all sailors in England are, for seven years before the mast. He had always been very polite in his attentions to us ladies, who were all the ladies on board; he courted our society at every leisure moment. My mother was so prepossessed with him that she made me mend all his clothes, for which favor he seemed grateful, and before our voyage was ended, made a declaration of love to myself. He wrote a letter and, when no one was observing, slipped it into my hand. This was a novelty I was not looking for. Every new object is pursued with avidity till familiarized by custom, and as that familiarity increases, it generally lessens in our esteem; nothing can gratify but possession.

6

Mr. Cotton proposed to marry me in Orleans, take me back on the same vessel and leave me with his parents, who were wealthy and had but two children, a daughter and a son. I had never given him any encouragement to address me, was rather cool in my politeness to him, and was much surprised on receiving the letter and reading the contents. I found an opportunity one evening to speak to him, told him my affections were already engaged. He was surprised and disappointed, and he could not have believed me, for he still continued his attentions where opportunity offered until they became unpleasant to me. I now stayed most of the time in his cabin and went on deck only when it was his turn to go below. My mother and sister plagued me so much about him that at times I was cross and sullen. The captain had been informed of my engagement to Henry by my mother, telling him at the same time that the father was a Jew, so that he continually called me the little Jewess, which added only to the great dislike I already felt for him. My mother and sister could always agree with him better than I could; although they did not like him, they would humor him and I would not.

A few days sail would bring us off the Island of Cuba. A small and suspicious-looking craft had been following us for several days. In the night we would out-sail her; in the morning we were always becalmed until mid-day when she would take up with us and be about two miles distant. We had no arms on board but one old swivel gun; a double-barreled gun bringing out for a gentleman in New Orleans, axes, and mauling spikes were all that were on board. There were eighteen men, sixteen sailors. Our captain told the deck passengers if we should be attacked they must fight for their lives. From the second day we saw them, my mother, sister and self were occupied in stowing out of sight, between decks, our clothing and valuables. My mother's jewelry, money, and some silk we put inside of our feather bed, which we threw carelessly up in our state room. Every vestige of clothing was hidden.

It was on Sunday morning, the 22nd day of April, 1832. On the seamen rising from their hammocks, they perceived our foes within a half a mile of us, coming with a speed that surprised all hands. There was not a breath of wind to be felt, and we lay completely becalmed. They had oars and were plying them with their might. It was a beautiful morning, and the sea shone with refulgent splendor, not a ruffle was on the sea; the fish were jumping out of the water, and several of them had been caught for breakfast. We ladies and the crew were called. On first seeing our enemies he arranged his crew, giving orders to be in readiness against the boat coming alongside. "Offer no resistance," said our captain, "unless you are obliged to. We have no other arms than that which the ship affords. I can see by my spy-glass there is about fifty men on deck, and perhaps fifty in the hold. If you are obliged to fight, then sell your lives as dearly as possible."

When the boat was close along our vessel, we were put into a secret closet by the captain, which had in it three shelves, kept expressly for the ship's papers and money and so concealed by the rest of the paneling that it could not be discovered. It opened and shut by a spring only known by the captain. After we were shut in, thought I, "What if this should be our last resting place?" My mother and sister were thinking the same. Should the captain get killed, no one that we knew of was informed of our hiding place. It was clear we could not remain there long without air, although he had promised to return as soon as he could and let us have air.

Whilst we waited in breathless agitation for his coming on board, I heard a voice say, "Have you no passengers?" "No cabin passengers; two men, steerage passengers." Presently I heard feet walking backwards and forwards in the cabin. At last the following conversation took place between our captain and the captain of the piratical schooner: "What is your cargo?" "Ballast only." "How much provisions?" "Not enough to last us to New Orleans." "I must have your provisions." "I cannot let you have it, sir; me and my men will starve if you do." "You will fall in with a vessel in a day or two who will supply you. You can take your choice or I will give you another. I will scuttle your vessel, then you will not need any provisions." With these last words dying upon his lips, he left the cabin and went on deck.

Our captain opened our door for a minute to take air and also went on deck. The pirates proceeded to rob and pillage the vessel of all the men's clothes and money, quadrants, and chronometers, and everything they found worth taking. Whilst they were thus employed, our men hid one barrel of bread and a small cask of water, but not without great difficulty, for they were watched upon every side of the vessel. It was impossible to contend with such a force as they had, from seventy to a hundred men. Whilst their craft was a very small one, not bigger than a fishing smack, they were a dark, designing set of cut throats, most of them Spaniards. Although our captain affirmed he met the captain of the piratical schooner before at some port, but he denied ever being there. They were armed to the teeth with pistols and long knives belted around them. Their captain looked English. He was asked why he did not hoist his signal when requested to do so. He replied that he did not carry but one flag and that was the black flag. "Shall I report you on our arrival in New Orleans?" Laughing and at the same time he replied, "D—— your report," and left for his own vessel.

As they were moving along side of us, the captain came to let us out of our hiding place. We were nearly choked for want of air, but must not look at our enemy until they were gone some distance from the vessel. Then the captain lent us his spy-glass to look at them through the cabin windows. A more blood-thirsty looking set of men I had never seen before, and although we were thankful at their departure, yet we did not know what would be our fate if we did not fall in with a vessel in a day or two, as we had been left without provisions and water. A man was immediately put at the mast head to look out for a sail.

I was cramped from my close confinement and had not regained the use of my feet, my face pale with fright.

My mother and sister wore the same appearance. For the first time I caught hold of the captain's arm and asked him what had transpired. With a countenance which bore marks of recent excitement, he replied to my impatient inquiries: "It was fortunate for you ladies that you were hid, and especially you, you little Jewess, for I feel certain that cut throat rascal would have carried you off with him. Then what would your lover do? Die in despair? They might have treated you badly. Death would be preferable. They have left us without provisions, and that is bad enough, but not as bad as if they had taken you ladies prisoners and in their power. They have taken my chronometer, and God knows how I am to steer my vessel. If we do not fall in with a ship in a day or two, we will starve to death before we can reach any land."

Ourselves and a crew were all put on an allowance of bread and water. One wine glass of water and one biscuit was our allowance a day, all sharing the same, passengers and crew. A flag of distress hung at the mast head, and we were traveling without knowing our exact course. All on board were cast down; the sailors looked sad, and not without reason. Our situation was one that might excite sympathy from the hardest heart. For myself, I felt resigned to my fate, knowing He who had delivered us from being wrecked upon the rocks was able to deliver us from death now. My mother tried to cheer us in our present situation. The captain kept sober; a man sat all day at the mast head to spy sail, for upon it is our lives depended.

In five days after the pirates boarded us, "A sail ahoy!" was shouted by the man at the mast head. Each heart leaped at the joyful news. In an hour afterwards, we could discover a sail. Another hour or two she was making for us. She came within speaking distance, asked what was wanted, when the captain asked him to come on board of us, as he had something to communicate. He came with the mate in the long boat. On telling him our situation and all that had befallen us, he sent us plenty of provisions, gave the captain a chronometer and all we wanted. It was the *Emerton* bound for Ireland, Captain Jones, with a rich cargo and considerable specie on board. This was the ship the pirates were watching, and being longer than they expected loading, the pirate vessel got out of provisions. Captain Jones, instead of going on, turned back and went to Balize,[3] mouth of the Mississippi River, where there was a man-of-war stationed, who went after the pirates and caught them; the captain and the chief officers were hung and the crew punished in accordance to law.

One night as we slept, we ran aground at the mouth of the Mississippi River. We remained here two days before we got off. A steam tug took us with another vessel

[3] A small village on stilts at the Gulf entrance to the Mississippi River was known as Balise or Balize. "Because the settlement was the first human thing seen in the Delta by inbound seafarers, vessels for New Orleans were commonly known as 'bound for Balize,' but the village eventually was abandoned and Pilot Town replaced it." The term comes from the French *balise* meaning "a beacon" or a signal for the guidance of buccaneers. Harold Sinclair, *The Port of New Orleans*, 267.

laden with fruit from Cuba. Next day we received an invitation to dine on board the Cuba schooner. We accepted it and were well entertained by some Spanish ladies who had noticed us on board the *St. George* and desired our company. They spoke good English, and I felt quite surprised at this, which made our visit more interesting. We had a good dinner, and when we left in the evening our captain returned the compliment by inviting them to supper. The ladies were good musicians and played on the guitar on which they sang well. I forgot to state that when off the Island of Cuba, a schooner came with fruit and shells to sell. I bought a good many beautiful shells, all of which I sent to Henry's mother. The Spanish ladies furnished us with fruit enough to last us several weeks, oranges and pineapples of the best quality, also bananas. They called on us a few days after our arrival in Orleans.

The first thing which attracted my attention in going up the Mississippi River was about young alligators sitting on a log, basking themselves in the sun. I felt as though I should be afraid to dwell amongst these reptiles. I saw one very large one, about ten feet long. I was surprised at his great length. I thought at first I should not like to live in this locality. But the beautiful Mississippi enchanted me, and the further we traveled up it the more I was delighted, my mother and sister also. I must not forget to tell my readers that none of us were sea sick. Only in the English Channel did we feel a little squeamish; and no wonder, for it was one continual gale whilst we were in it.

On our arrival at Orleans, a gentleman by the name

of Alexander MacCaulah came on board to receive letters. Our captain introduced us.

I must now say something about our costume which was the established mode of dress for young ladies when we left England, and notwithstanding its singularity, was becoming to a good figure. Brown and green broadcloth dresses, and the finest quality of cloth, the brown embroidered with red and green worsted in flowers down the front and up the skirt, round the bottom. The green were made the same, only braided with black silk braid in flowers. A cape of black silk pointed behind and before, and lapels laid over the front. Bonnets of black silk, the brim wide in front and tapering off behind; a plume of ostrich feathers hung over the front of our bonnets. I must tell you that our dresses were made so short that they reached just a little below the knees; handsome pantelettes trimmed with rich pointed lace, high made gaiters, cloth-tops and fastened on the side. This finished our costumes. The citizens would gaze at us as we passed in the streets, and we would often hear them say, "How pretty!" "They are foreigners." Gentlemen would touch their hats in recognition and make way for us to pass. On entering the theatre at night, a round of applause greeted our ears. The newspapers were full of compliments to my mother and two daughters, the week of our arrival, in giving an account of the accident which happened to us in running so near the Island of Neves, with our piratical adventure. They spoke of us as brave girls and women, firm in the hour of danger. I thought if our reporter had seen us in the closet with our faces white with fear, he would not have sacrificed truth to politeness. He also praised our complexions, our figures, eyes, and hair, and concluded with saying if the young gentlemen of Orleans could keep their hearts whole whilst we remained, they must be more than mother earth.

The city of Orleans was a small town at this time, and but three or four streets worth notice, in which were the principal residences;[4] fronting the Mississippi River were the principal business houses, the wharf, and warehouses. The ships laid along side of the wharf and were convenient for lading.

On being invited out to dine one day, a plate of cornbread was handed to me. I took a piece not knowing what it was; it was light as a sponge cake, and until my mother informed me what it was, I took it to be a pudding. It was the first I had ever tasted; cannot say I fancied it much at that time. Have since learned to eat cornbread and like it.

The morning came for us to leave Orleans. Mr. MacCaulah . . . for several days previous to our leaving had been laying in a supply of dainties for our voyage: cake and fruit, a beautiful crepe shawl, and many other smaller presents, which, as I refused to accept them, he gave in

[4] In 1832 New Orleans was a city of 42,000 and a municipality "invested with extensive powers to lay out streets, improve public places, and develop the suburbs." John Smith Kendall, *History of New Orleans*, II, 132.

charge to my mother, with instructions not to give them to me until I landed in Texas. He asked me if I would not write him on my getting to my journey's end. I promised to do so by way of getting rid of his importunities. Mr. George Johnston made me a present of a valuable set of jewelry, which he had purchased for the lady who deceived him in marrying another man. It cost 40 dollars, breast pin and ear rings. They were enclosed in a beautiful leather case lined with purple velvet. I objected to receiving them, but on being pressed by his sister, I did so. He said he could not bear to see them, or he would have given them to his sister. John, my favorite, gave me a beautiful tortoise shell music box. It played ten tunes. I thought much of this present, as I was passionately fond of music; besides, John was the only youth I was interested in, without being in love.

All of our friends went down to the vessel to see us off. It had rained a little that day, and the streets were very muddy. In wet weather it was a perfect mud hole, very sickly, and a graveyard from the deaths that took place daily.

After taking leave of all our New Orleans friends, the vessel started down the river. At the mast head of a vessel might be seen two or three young gentlemen wringing their pocket handkerchiefs under pretense of being wet with tears. They waved their hats and handkerchiefs several times, kissed their hands, and this was their final adieu.

Several gentlemen on board the *Sabine*[5] had noticed them and said, "I presume those ladies have left their hearts behind. How unfortunate for us bachelors." My mother and sister and self kept the deck until late in the evening, until we felt we had got our sea-legs, as the sailors term it. We had been over five weeks off the water, and as soon as we got out in the Gulf of Mexico it made us feel a little squeamish, but we were none of us sea sick. We had a good joke on the gentlemen on board, who expected to see us retire to the cabin as soon as we got out in the Gulf, but when we continued to pace the deck in conversation with the captain, they were not a little surprised. We heard the following conversation take place between two of the gentlemen, who I afterwards learned were a Mr. Stanford and Mr. McNeil:[6] "I think them girls must be

[5] The schooner *Sabine* figured prominently in operations along the Texas coast in pre-Revolution days. An advertisement on page two of the Saturday, June 15, 1833, issue of *The Constitutional Advocate and Texas Public Advertiser* informed the public: "SAILED . . . Schooner Sabine, Brown, for New Orleans, crossed the bar on Tuesday." Travis L. Smith, Jr., in "Steamboats on the Brazos," in *A History of Brazoria County, Texas* (ed. by T. L. Smith), 65, identifies the *Sabine* merely as a schooner that ran the blockade at Velasco, and Jim Dan Hill mentions that "Ugartechea was already so thoroughly over-awed by rowdy Brazorians that ships came and went, such as the defiant schooner *Sabine*, with or without permission." Hill, *The Texas Navy*, 12.

[6] Sterling McNeel was owner of Darrington Plantation, on which was erected a substantial frame residence, slave cabins, and a double set of sugar kettles. He was one of four brothers, three of whom, with a cousin, Pinckney McNeel, participated in the battle of San Ja-

made of something extra. Whilst we poor fellows are casting up our accounts, they seem perfectly well and as much at home as a duck in water." "Yes," replied Mr. McNeil, "and I feel not a little ashamed that I, a stronger vessel, am compelled to lie here on my back and allow the captain to monopolize all their company. Fine looking girl, that oldest one, fine eyes, fine form, and the other is also a very interesting girl. What are their names?" "Oh, there you have me; the captain is selfish, he has not yet introduced them to any one on board. I think he has a liking for the oldest one of the girls, but I'll cut him out when I get on land, so he had better make good use of his time."

In another hour, no one but the seamen, mother, sister, and self and captain on deck; all gone below sea sick. After being on board a day or two the captain said, "Ladies, I had expected to make your passage money clear,

---

cinto. Abner Strobel, *Old Plantations and Their Owners of Brazoria County, Texas*, 52.

Rutherford B. Hayes, who visited Texas in 1847, wrote in his diary Tuesday, January 30:

Ride with Mr. [James E.] Perry over to Sterling McNeal's plantation. A shrewd, intelligent, cynical old bachelor, full of "wise saws and modern instances"; very fond of telling his own experience and talking of his own affairs. Living alone he has come to think he is the "be all' and "end all" here. The haughty and imperious part of a man develops rapidly on one of these lonely sugar plantations, where the owner rarely meets with any except his slaves and minions.

Charles Richard Williams, *The Life of Rutherford Birchard Hayes, Nineteenth President of the United States*, I, 50.

but instead of that you will consume it all!" "I am glad," I replied, "you got disappointed."

Captain Brown[7] did everything to make our passage agreeable, and not until we had been on board three days did he introduce us to the gentlemen passengers, who I understand were very anxious to be acquainted with us. One evening, on being called to supper, I saw opposite a gentleman who was extremely sober looking, who kept his eyes fixed upon myself continually. I took him for a Methodist preacher and asked the captain if he was not one. He laughed heartily and said, "No, that is Mr. McN, one of our wealthiest planters. If you were acquainted

---

[7] William S. Brown, a brother of Jeremiah Brown, captain of the *Invincible*, was named master of the schooner *Liberty* and on March 3, 1836, captured the Mexican trading vessel *Pelicano* and delivered its cargo to Matagorda Bay. After a quarrel with Charles E. Hawkins, commodore of the Texas Navy, he was relieved of his command of the *Liberty*, but in July, 1836, received another naval commission, taking charge of two captured Mexican vessels, the *Comanche* and the *Fanny Butler*. Later, he was named captain of the privateer *Benjamin R. Milam* but died in New Orleans before the ship was ready for service. Webb, *The Handbook of Texas*, I, 226.

Brown was a resident of Velasco and took part in the siege of Bexar, but after the capitulation of Cos, he went to Goliad, where he is said to have designed the revolutionary flag showing the bloody arm, stripes of red and white, and the word Independence embroidered on it. This flag was hoisted at Velasco in January, 1836.

William's brother Jeremiah was captain of the *Liberty* and later of the Invincible. when the American brig *Pocket*, loaded with supplies for the Mexican Army, was captured. After the battle of San Jacinto, Brown went to New Orleans to get supplies but was arrested for piracy of the *Pocket*. His crew was released, but the captain's personal difficulties resulted in his replacement as commander. *Ibid.*, I, 225.

with him, you would find him quite communicative and intelligent." I asked the captain if he would not introduce me to him, which he did half an hour afterward. I was agreeably disappointed in Mr. McN. I found him a man well informed, polite, and witty. He seldom laughed, and when talking, as serious as a judge. As I became better acquainted I liked him much more. I became interested in him.

One morning, quite suddenly, we struck the bar off the mouth of the Brazos River, which gave the vessel such a shock as to throw us all down that were on deck. I sprained my ankle very bad. We struck two more times and were over. I was much alarmed, thought we were all going to pieces, at least the ship. There was a German doctor on board, who bandaged my ankle, but I could not walk for the space of two weeks without a stick. That morning we anchored in the Brazos River. Our voyage of two weeks had been a favorable one. The wind being unfavorable for the vessel to go up the river, in a short time after we anchored in the river, Mr. McN came to bid us goodbye. "I will see you again, ladies, on your arrival at Brazoria." I was struck with this information. A small boat was alongside which he stept into with two other gentlemen. One a Mr. Anthony,[8] editor of the paper at

[8] D. W. Anthony was editor of *The Constitutional Advocate and Texas Public Advertiser*, published in Brazoria. He advertised in his own paper that he was an attorney-at-law, capable of giving "the strictest and most faithful attention to all matters of litigation confided to his management. Letters addressed to him, and persons calling to see him on business, will find him at BRAZORIA, where he is located

Brazoria, the other Mr. Randon,[9] brother-in-law to Mr. McN. All these gentlemen had given us invitations to visit them on our arrival at Brazoria; Mr. John Austin[10] was another passenger, all planters, and some whose names I have forgotten. When they left the schooner it seemed strange to me, who was unacquainted with the locality of the country, how they could go 30 miles through the woods that looked unpenetrable. I had never beheld such

permanently." *The Constitutional Advocate and Texas Public Advertiser*, June 15, 1833. Anthony died of cholera in July, 1833. Webb, *The Handbook of Texas*, I, 53.

[9] John Randon, one of Austin's Old Three Hundred, received title to a *sitio* of land in present Fort Bend County. The March, 1826, census lists him as a farmer and stock raiser between twenty-five and forty years of age and with a household consisting of a wife, two sons, and thirteen slaves. His plantation was a log cabin, kitchen, stables, and seventy acres of land under fence on the east side of the Brazos River, twenty miles below San Felipe. His wife was Nancy McNeel, a daughter of John McNeel and sister of L. H., Sterling, John, Pleasant, George, and Elizabeth McNeel.

[10] John Austin was a native of Connecticut. Going to sea as a youth, he was in New Orleans in 1819 and joined the Long Expedition. As a member of the Long group, he was taken to Mexico as a prisoner and upon release contacted Stephen F. Austin. It is believed that the two men were distantly related; they did form a close personal friendship, and in 1832, John joined Stephen at San Felipe, working with him in settling the original colonists. John Austin served as constable for the district of San Felipe de Austin and, financed by Stephen, formed a partnership with J. E. B. Austin, younger brother of the empresario, in operating a mercantile business at Brazoria. He enlarged his business interests to include cattle and shipping. He served as port authority, was appointed alcalde, and was a delegate to the Convention of 1832. He participated in the Anahuac disturbances, the Battle of Velasco, and the Turtle Bayou Resolutions. Webb, *The Handbook of Texas*, I, 81.

timber before, with their beautiful green leaves and whose blossoming shrubs perfumed the air.

The wind still being contrary for us to get up the river with the schooner, captain became impatient, so took the yawl boat and started up the river with us, leaving the vessel in charge of the mate. Two Spaniards rowed us in the boat. On going up the river, we stopped at a Mr. Bertrand's plantation[11] and got some buttermilk, the first I had drunk since we left England, which was very grateful to us all. Milk in New Orleans was one-half chalk, the other half water, so my readers can imagine how we enjoyed it. We camped one night on the river bank, where we liked to have been eat up by the mosquitoes. It was precious little sleeping we did that night. I would first look at the forest and then the river and thought I would be a dainty morsel for the alligators, which were constantly leaping out of the water, or the panthers who were making night hideous with their cries. At a short distance from my mother and sister I sat, reclining on my hand, full of thought of the past and future. My

[11] Ann Raney probably refers to Peter Gabriel Bertrand, whose league of land, abstract no. 42, was on the east bank of the Brazos just above the town of Velasco and approximately seven and one-half air miles from the mouth of the river. (A map owned by Mrs. L. G. Rich shows the location of the plantation.) Bertrand ran an advertisement in *The Telegraph and Texas Register* on September 23, 1837, offering a reward of one hundred dollars for apprehension of Arthur and George, two slaves. He indicated that the Negros could be delivered to him "on the Brazos timbers, three miles above colonel Hall's plantation." Arthur, he explained, "left my plantation on Sept. 12." The dateline on the advertisement was Evergreen.

mother was trying to sleep, which she at last found to be impossible.

Everyone was glad to see the day come. An early breakfast was prepared, and we left our camp ground before sun up. I took a few clothes in a hand box, enough to last me till the vessel should arrive. The boat being leaky, the bottom came out, and my case of jewelry which Mr. Johnston gave me was gone. The captain searched the boat and every place that he thought of. The Spaniards denied seeing them, or having any knowledge about them. This was a cross to me which I did not get over easily, but took it easily at the time, as I did not wish to hurt the captain's feelings, as he was already much put out of humor. He always believed the Spaniards secreted them.

At five o'clock in the evening, we arrived at the town of Brazoria.[12] A voice saluted my ear from the bank, "I

[12] A traveler visiting Texas in March, 1831, "to examine the condition of a large tract of land I had purchased of the Galveston Bay and Texas Land Company," describes Brazoria as containing

about thirty houses, all of logs except three of brick and two or three framed, and several more were building. It is laid out in squares of an eighth of an acre. The river was now about twenty feet lower than the street, but is swollen every year so much during the seasons of floods, as to rise, nearly to the same level, and indeed sometimes overflows a part of it. The soil was here, as below, very rich bottom land, black, and 20 feet deep. It is probable that Brazoria will be the head of sloop navigation; for although the river above is for some distance deep enough for vessels of that class, its crooked course presents a great objection to proceeding any further up the channel unless with oars. Lots of one-eighth of an acre sold at from twenty to one hundred and

am glad to see you." On looking up I saw Mr. McN. I felt glad to see him. He helped us one by one get out of the boat, seizing my arm first as I could only walk by the aid of a stick. My mother next. He went with us to the hotel, leaving the captain to bring my sister, which he did as soon as he gave some directions to the men in the boat. He spent the rest of the evening with us. The landlady and her daughter,[13] who was married, Mrs. W

---

forty dollars. Brazoria is thirty miles up the river, but 45 miles by its crooked course.

Visit to Texas, Being the Journal of a Traveller, 30.

[13] Born in Maryland on July 23, 1798, the seventh child of Captain William Mackall Wilkinson and Anne Herbert Dent Wilkinson, Jane Wilkinson Long became known as the "Daughter of Maryland, Wife of Mississippi, and the Mother of Texas." When she was thirteen years of age, she moved to Washington, Mississippi Territory, and lived at Propinquity Plantation with an older sister. Wounded men of the War of 1812, one of whom was Dr. James Long, flocked to the plantation. A territorial law required an orphan, upon reaching a certain age, to select a guardian; Jane Wilkinson selected Dr. Long.

Dr. Long and his charge were married May 14, 1815. A daughter was born on November 26, 1816, and when she was fifteen, Anne Herbert Long was sent to school in Natchez, where she met and married Edward Winston in January, 1832. In April, the couple joined Mrs. Long at Matagorda, Texas. With a man in the family again, Mrs. Long took up her grant on the site of Old Fort Bend, but later in 1832 she opened in Brazoria the boarding house which became famous in history.

She ran it for five years, and she and Kian [her faithful slave] did all the work, even the laundry. Here Stephen F. Austin delivered his keynote address to the Convention of 1835. This was followed by a visit from Colonel Juan N. Almonte with a great flourish of trumpets, and Jane Long was taking part in the intrigues of the time. While Almonte traded compliments with

gave us a warm reception, had a good supper, our hostess making herself very agreeable. Mrs. L was a widow, one of the early day settlers, was anxious for emigration to the country, and was very polite to strangers, kept a good table, and had a great deal of customers.

The country was full of bachelors,[14] but very few ladies. When bed[time] came we were ushered into a room where there were several beds. We did not like this much, as we expected a room to ourselves, but on being told that the gentlemen slept on one side and the ladies on the other side of the room, I opened both my eyes and ears and looked again at my hostess, who did not seem to be jesting. Presently several more ladies came in to go to bed. They went through the undressing operation quickly and were

his hosts in the dining room, secretly taking notes on the resources of the country, the entertainers were procuring powder and arms and storing them in a brick outhouse on Jane's place.

After the death of Edward Winston, Anne married Judge J. S. Sullivan. Anne A. Brindley, "Jane Long," *The Southwestern Historical Quarterly*, LVI, 2, 237.

[14] A scarcity of women existed on the frontier. A visitor to Texas in 1837 whose name is unknown observed that on the anniversary of the Battle of San Jacinto, 1837, "as Houston could not furnish a sufficient number of ladies, there was to be a general beating of the bushes along the Brazos, Oyster and Caney creeks to make up the necessary complement." A footnote to the manuscript adds, " . . . in this place, that, in the whole population of Houston, I doubt whether there were more than sixty or seventy females, both married and single. Some of the immigrants had left their wives behind until the country became more settled, and many had never had any. For the benefit of the ladies, I would mention that speculations are to be made in Texas." Andrew Forest Muir (ed.), *Texas in 1837*, 42.

all in bed long before we had got over our surprise at this new fashion of sleeping. We soon undressed but did not divest ourselves of all our garments, keeping on outside garments which were calico wrappers. We had been in bed about an hour when the gentlemen came in one by one until all had retired. I watched with breathless suspense the coming of the last one. This was something we were not accustomed to, and it was several nights before I could sleep—not until nature was completely exhausted and overcome with watching.

The ladies all laughed at us and said, "By the time you have been in Texas a few months, if you travel in the country, you will have to sleep with the man and his wife at the house you visit," as houses were only log cabins with two rooms, one for the house servants, the other for the family. I found this statement correct, visiting some friends in the country two weeks after this who had a small log cabin with two rooms in it, the servants and cooking one, the other to sleep in. I had to sleep with the man and his wife. I slept at the back of the bed, the wife in the middle and the man in front. They were settlers, had gone into the woods to make a plantation, and this was considered a shelter for the present. They worked thirty hands, and several negroes lived together in one cabin. This was the way most of the wealthy planters lived when we first arrived in Texas. A double log cabin with an entry running through the middle was their residence. To make money was their chief object, all things else were subsidiary to it.

Mrs. L's house was crowded every day with strangers out of the country; three or four tables set at meal hours. Many came through curiosity to see the "Belles with the Breeches" as they called my sister and self. Night after night, Mrs. L's house was open for a dancing party. We, being good dancers and our dress every way suited our figures and to show our feet, were the chief attraction, there being few young ladies in the country. Those parties were very social, and my sister and self enjoyed ourselves much. My sister had several admirers, as well as myself.

After a few days rest from our voyage, we started out on horseback to see my father, who was living at Mr. Bailey's,[15] about seven or eight miles from Brazoria.

[15] James Briton Bailey, a native of North Carolina, came to Texas with his wife Nancy and six children by April, 1821, settling near the Brazos River on what became known as Bailey's Prairie. His squatter's claim, legalized July 7, 1824, brought Bailey recognition as one of Austin's Old Three Hundred.

When the settlers convened to take the oath of fidelity to the Convention of 1824, they met with Austin at Bailey's home, and during the meeting Bailey was named lieutenant of a company of militia. Webb, *The Handbook of Texas*, I, 95.

Bailey died about 1833 and, the story is told, was buried standing erect, a rifle at his side, a jug of whiskey at his feet, and a powder horn strapped over his shoulders with lead bullets ready to load. He was interred facing west, having said that all his life he had gone westward, and when he awakened he wished to be headed in that familiar direction. Mary Nixon Rogers, "A History of Brazoria County, Texas," in Smith, *A History of Brazoria County, Texas*, 47.

"As unconventional in death as he was in life, Brit was buried as he directed—standing erect and facing the west. Storytellers could not resist adding a picturesque phrase, 'with his gun at his side and his jug at his feet.'" Kim S. Garrett, "Family Stories and Sayings," *Singers and Storytellers*, XXX, 277.

Captain Brown was our escort. We arrived there in time for dinner. Although my father was expecting us, yet we took him by surprise, not hearing of our arrival at Brazoria. Many tears of joy were shed on all sides. Even Mr. Bailey and his family were affected to tears, and our brave captain was seen to dash a tear away also. We were shocked to survey my father's person; he was but the shadow of his former self. A man of seventy years would not have looked any older, yet he was not forty-five; his flesh gone, eyes sunk, bent form, he was in the worst state of health. Nevertheless he taught Mr. Bailey's children during this time, as their education was very limited. We stayed with him a few days and returned to Mrs. L's hotel, as Mr. B's house was small enough for his own family, until my father could get a house for us in town, which was very difficult to do in those times. Every new settler had to put up his own house.

After being one month at the hotel, we got two rooms next to the printing office, also a kitchen to cook in. This was a favor, and we were glad to go to housekeeping so as to be all together and out of the bustle and noise of hotel life. I was tired of being primped and dressed to receive visitors, which were not a few, both in town and country, that called on us. After we came to Brazoria we found many new acquaintances and many warm friends. . . . One, Mr. McN, who had always been deeply interested for our welfare, happiness, and comfort. He never proposed for my hand, much less my heart. He often said, "I wish you to consider me your best friend." He was far from being good looking, but very interesting, his eyes keen and penetrating. He never said he loved me. If he had, then our friendship would have ended. I looked upon him more as a brother than a friend. I confided to him all my secrets and sorrows. He was seldom my escort, and none suspected he had ever enlisted my sympathies.

Captain B was my constant companion, walking, riding out for an airing; everyone said we were engaged to be married, and although unremitting in his attentions he had not proposed marriage. He had been bold enough to ask my mother and father for my hand, but had kept the strictest silence upon this subject to myself. Captain B was a great favorite with my mother. She thought him par-excellence. I admit of one thing; he had been a warm friend of our family and had been much service to us on our landing in Texas. He introduced us to many families of the first standing and brought us many things from Orleans which we could not get in Texas. He was a general favorite amongst ladies and welcome visitor in every family. He was a Bostonian by birth, six foot high, fair hair and complexion, light eyes, very good looking, fine address. He was a handsome gallant, fond of dress and neat in person. He lived a good deal at our house, eating two meals out of three every day. Would have liked him better had I not seen quite so much of him. He was always teasing me or my sister with being called the Belles with the Breeches. I was not indifferent to him, but I liked Mr. McN better.

*Ann's mother strongly voiced her hope that Ann would
accept Captain Brown's proposal of marriage. Ann's father,
however, comforted his distraught daughter, saying, "Never,
my child, will I compel you to marry any man against your
will. My house is always your home, and if your mother is
angry, she will soon get over it and be sorry for what she has
said. Your happiness is mine. Captain is a fine man. If you
cannot like him as a husband, you can as a friend."*

*Nevertheless, Ann resolved to visit D. R, approximately
nine miles from Brazoria, and make clear to him her situation.
At five o'clock one midsummer evening, on a borrowed side-
saddle and horse, she left for Brazoria.*

*The following morning, Ann entered the breakfast room
to find the family assembled. Among those at the table was
Mr. McN, who laughed at Ann's surprise. "A little bird
came this morning and informed me of your arrival at my
sister's, and I have come to eat breakfast with you."*

Mr. S. McN was a constant visitor at his sister's,
Mrs. R's. One evening late we were told that there was a
cannon heard down the river. Everyone was in motion.
"To Arms," was the cry, and in less than a few hours the
men from every part of the country had gone to the scene
of action. Some of our merchant vessels had passed the
fort, refusing to pay duties at the custom house to the
Mexican authorities, and when fired on by the Mexican
soldiers, this was a signal for an outbreak.[16] In three days

[16] The Battle of Velasco on June 26, 1832, brought the first
bloodshed in the relations between Texas and Mexico. Lieutenant Colonel Dominio Ugartechea, commander of Fort Velasco, under orders of
Colonel John Bradburn, refused to permit the Texans on the Brazos

we took the fort, after killing one hundred and wounding two hundred, taking the rest prisoners, which I understood was some two thousand men. Mrs. R and myself sat the most of two nights and days moulding bullets and making bullet patches. The ladies in Brazoria were occupied in the same way for two days and nights. Captain W. B, I was told, behaved with a reckless bravery, standing at the cannon and firing every shot himself as long as the battle lasted. The bullets flew around his person by the

to transport artillery past the mouth of the river. Aroused by John Austin, Henry S. Brown, William J. Russell, Dr. Charles B. Stewart, and George B. McKinstry, the people of Brazoria armed themselves, secured the schooner *Brazoria*, and prepared to sail to Anahuac. On June 25, the Texans, commanded by John Austin, demanded formal surrender of Fort Velasco. When the demand was disregarded, Austin's men prepared to attack.

The 112 men were organized into one marine and two infantry companies under Russell, Brown, and Austin. On board the *Brazoria*, Russell, with two small cannon, a blunderbuss, and eighteen riflemen, planned to draw abreast of the fort and moor near the bank. Brown would detour to the east and "effect a lodgement behind the drift logs." Austin would approach from the north. By opening fire, Brown was to draw the Mexicans' fire, thus permitting Austin's men to take their positions behind cypress palisades, but an accidental shot by one of Brown's men revealed the troops, and the battle began.

The Texans marched within twenty-five paces of the fort and were exposed, but the artillery in the fort was aimed toward the schooner. "At one time during the fight the Texan fire from the schooner was so fatal, that the Mexicans rushed out of the fort to take the vessel, but the fire of the besiegers from the land-side drove them back with loss." Eleven hours after the bloody conflict began, the Mexicans hoisted a white flag, and, deprived of their arms, were set free. John Henry Brown, *History of Texas*, I, 181–85. Henderson Yoakum, *History of Texas From Its Settlement in 1685 to Its Annexation to the United States in 1846*, 294–95.

hundreds, yet he escaped unharmed. Colonel Williams[17] lost his eye in the battle, Mr. Sanders[18] was wounded in the arm. Mr. Williams[19] of the town of Brazoria was the only man killed on our side, and some few others wounded slightly.

This battle was the beginning of the future strife, for General St. Anna, on hearing of this massacre of his men, sent one of his generals to Brazoria[20] to make terms with

[17] Robert H. Williams of Caney, John Henry Brown reports, lost an eye while serving in the second company under Captain Henry S. Brown. Brown, *History of Texas*, I, 186. *The Handbook of Texas* (II, 914) notes that Williams "had an eye put out by a splinter" in the battle. Williams lived on a plantation on Caney Creek, and there he built the third cotton gin erected in Texas.

[18] The name Sanders does not appear in the rolls of men serving under Austin, Russell, or Brown, yet 13 of the 112 men who took part in the Battle of Velasco remain unidentified. Brown, *History of Texas*, I, 186.

[19] Jesse Williams and Job Williams of the Navidad, who served in Brown's company, are possibilities, yet Ann may refer to one of the thirteen unknown who participated in the battle. Yoakum reports that Texan losses were 7 killed and 27 wounded. The Mexicans suffered 37 killed and 15 wounded. Yoakum, *History of Texas*, 294–95.

The Handbook of Texas (II, 836) gives the strength of Texas forces as between 100 and 150 and the Mexican troops between 100 and 150. This source lists Texas casualties as 7 killed and 14 wounded, 3 of them dying later. The Mexicans had 5 killed and 16 wounded.

[20] Shortly after the Battle of Velasco, "Colonel Mexia was dispatched with his fleet to Velasco for the purpose of investigating the disturbance in this part of the Mexican nation. Feeling that the presence of Stephen F. Austin would influence, and thus contribute to the calming of the colonists, Mexia officially invited Austin to accompany him. After hearing a full report from John Austin, and deliberating with Stephen F. Austin, Mexia proceeded to Brazoria, where he was honored at a gala reception and a grand ball at the

our people in a treaty, which ended in giving a dinner and ball at night. His ambassador returned to Mexico, and General St. Anna renewed his force, and in '36 he returned with a force of 10,000 men. I was invited to the ball and danced with General Urea (Mexia S.E.) and some Spanish gentlemen of note, Stephen F. Austin, the Empresario of Texas. I was much complimented on my being a good dancer, and the Empresario was so much pleased with me, having been in conversation with him some time, that on learning I was the daughter of John R of England, next day my father received a note from him to wait on him and he would give him another league

tavern of Mrs. Jane Long, the charming and courageous widow of Dr. James Long, of the ill-fated Long expedition. There were speeches appropriate to the occasion, interspersed with toasts to Mexia and Austin, and good will was once again established between the Mexican government and the colonists." Rogers, in Smith, *A History of Brazoria County, Texas*, 65.

José Antonio Mexía, by his own account, was born in Jalapa, although many contemporary writers state that he was a Cuban. From November, 1829, to January, 1831, he was secretary to the Mexican legation in the United States, and in June and July, 1832, directed a Federalist expedition from Tampico to subdue the Centralist forces in Matamoros. From Matamoros he was accompanied by Stephen F. Austin on what is known as Mexía's Expedition Across Texas. During the trip he became convinced of Texas' loyalty to Mexico. On this expedition Mexía had four hundred troops when he crossed the Brazos River on July 16, to be hospitably received by the residents of Brazoria. In a meeting on July 17, he listened to them explain the cause of the disturbances. After a six-day stay in Brazoria, Mexía was satisfied with events and went to Galveston, where, on July 24, he met vessels bearing the troops from Anahuac. Convinced that Texas affairs were progressing, he sailed. Webb, *The Handbook of Texas*, II, 182–83.

of land, his first being taken from him because father did not join him as soon as was required by Mr. Austin, as it was two years instead of one before we joined him. My father went and received his grant before the Empresario left town.

I still attended balls and places of amusement with Mr. R or Mr. S. McN as my escorts. I met my sister once after I left home, but never with my father and mother. My sister, in tears, asked me to return, said she thought my mother was sorry for what she had said. I told her to give my love to her father, and say I still loved them as a daughter. My sister wished me to go home with her, but I did not do so. My mother's health was not good at this time. She was undergoing her acclimating and had fever quite often. My father's health declined every day and got worse. He seldom ever went out, only when his health permitted him to do so. I felt as though I had seen him for the last time. I dared not go home to see him and I was much troubled about him. I felt I should like to plead once more for her forgiveness, but this was not to be. God had determined otherwise. My sister, on parting, begged me to marry Captain Brown, but on telling her I did not love him well enough to make him my husband, though she seemed displeased at the moment, she kissed me on parting.

I was so homesick to see my parents, I sank under oppression of spirits, and in a week after seeing my sister I was taken with bilious and remitting fever. For three weeks there was no change for the better. Two physicians were in attendance. They gave me up. They could do no more for me. I might linger a few days longer, but all medicine had lost its affect.

I had known no one for a week, and when the doctors left me to die, Mr. S. McN and Mrs. R still continued to give me medicine and at last succeeding in salivating me, which my physicians had tried to do but had not been successful.

I was spared for other troubles. Everything was done for my comfort by the family and my best friend, Mr. S. McN. I was so badly salivated that for several weeks I held my head in a position for the saliva to run out, which was nearly out of bed. Pieces of flesh half as long as my finger would fall off the inside of my mouth. My food was boiled milk thickened with flour. This was all I was allowed for several weeks. I often cried with pain it gave me to eat it, and I often cried with hunger. I was only allowed by my physician one pint at a meal. I could have drank a quart.

I must state a circumstance which occurred one day when Mrs. R and her family were not at home. As I did not gain strength fast I thought it was because I did not get enough to eat. I tried to walk, but found I could not hold out to the kitchen, so I got down on my knees and crawled. The black woman saw me and said, "Miss Ann, are you going to kill yourself? Where are you going?" "No," I replied, "but I might as well die one way as another. I am starving to death for want of something to eat, and I want you to give me a potato." "Lord bless

35

your pale face, it is more than my life is worth to give you any more than you are allowed." "I must have it, cook, or I cannot get well." "I dare not give it to you; my mistress will kill me if it should hurt you."

I knew there were potatoes cooking in the oven for dinner, so I opened the stove door and took the first one I could find and was crawling off in triumph with my prize when the cook came and lifted me in her arms and carried me to my room. "If it does not hurt you, Miss Ann, to eat that potato, I will let you have one every day until the family will allow you to eat them." "If it kills me," I said, "I will never tell." I devoured my potato with eagerness little short of hunger. From this hour I got better. Next day, and for several days after, the cook brought me another potato, for which act she had my warmest thanks. I was now getting better daily. My appetite knew no bounds, and I was cautioned by Mr. R not to eat too much.

I was now an orphan with neither father nor mother to bless my return to health. It was during my illness that my mother and sister were taken sick, my father already confined to his bed. I was sent for in their dying moments, but could not go. I was also given up by my physician. Mrs. R would not tell me of their deaths whilst I lay low. Before life was gone, my dear mother told my sister if she lived to get well, to tell me that she forgave me, and that perhaps it was all for the best that I did not comply with her request in marrying Captain W. B. My mother died nine days before my father. My sister, after my father's and mother's deaths, went to live with Mrs. Chase at

Velasco,[21] at the mouth of the Brazos River, remaining at the hotel with Mrs. L until she recovered her health. Mrs. L and her daughter were very kind to her, and she had many warm friends.

I now took a walk every day to gain strength. I was delighted with all I saw of the woods and prairies. The beautiful wild flowers of Texas cannot be surpassed. In these shades of solitude, I had leisure for reflection of past and present, but dared not look far into the perspective. I could not disperse the gloom that pervaded my whole nature, and in those seasons of retirement I alone sheltered my weary spirit.

As soon as I was able to ride, I went to the town of Brazoria to see my sister. Our meeting inflicted a fresh wound to our hearts. My sister was not strong enough to leave her room or bed. She was wasted in person and emaciated, her eyes sunk, her cheeks pale. We laid plans for us to be together. I proposed teaching a school, but in naming it to our friends they would not consent to it, saying we were too young. After staying a day or so with her, I took leave of her for a short season, telling her I would return in a few days. My sister and self were doubly dear to each other now. We were orphans. My sole thought was to make a home for my sister, who had always been my mother's favorite, being the youngest child and a delicate one. She missed my mother, and it was

[21] Possibly the wife of William Chase, who operated a hotel at the mouth of the Brazos. Duncan W. Robinson, *Texas 3-Legged Willie*, 15.

with difficulty I sought to console her grief. I told her we should not always be separated. I said the first chance I had of making myself a good home, she could come to live with me. She smiled sorrowfully and replied, "Do not be hasty in your choice on my account; look well before you leap."

Mr. S. McN was much distressed at his father's injunction if he married he would disinherit him. Mrs. R had to run away and get married, also Mr. G. McN, another one of his sons, so that he was not willing for any of his sons to marry.[22] Mrs. R told me, "All the rest of the family are willing for you to marry my brother, with whom you are a great favorite and with my father himself, but he was never willing for his children to marry."

I was in my room one evening when I overheard the following conversation pass between Mr. R and his brother-in-law, Mr. S. McN. "If you still wish to marry Miss Ann, I will make her a present of a horse and saddle and you had best run off and get married, as your father will only be angry for a time, as he has been with all the rest." Mr. S. McN observed, "My father's health is very

---

[22] "Old Mr. McNeel" was Johnny McNeel, who "didn't want any of his children to marry, but to stay there with him till he died. . . . He ran Nancy off when she married David Randon and John Greenville, too, when he married Ann Westall. Pleasant never married, nor Sterling. Old Leander waited till Old Johnnie died. I think Leander was oldest, then Pleasant, or Nancy. George W. died unmarried. Elizabeth married Robt. Mills." Dr. Samuel E. Asbury to Harriet E. Smither, October 2, 1945, Asbury Papers, Texas State Library Archives.

bad, and he cannot live long, and I think it best to wait awhile longer until he is dead. Miss Ann is young enough yet to marry and has a good home, and she shall not want for anything. I wish you to tell her my intentions."

When Mrs. R informed me what her brother desired her to tell me, I was silent; seeing I did not reply, she said, "My brother S loves money and does not wish my father to disinherit him, as he has always been a great favorite with him." Mr. S. McN came about once a week to see me, and sometimes, once in two weeks. This was quite a change for me who had been accustomed to seeing him once a day, and he sometimes remained all day. I felt hurt at his seeming neglect and all my former pride returned. "He does not love," I thought, "or he would not mind his father's injunction. He loves his father's money better than me."

I went to spend the day with Mrs. Munson,[23] a neighbor of Mrs. R and an excellent woman. I met with Miss Emeline W[24] at her house, a young lady who was

[23] Henry Munson operated a cotton and sugar plantation situated on Gulf Prairie. Abner J. Strobel, *Old Plantations and Their Owners of Brazoria County, Texas*, 9. Munson witnessed the fight between Emeline Westall and Ann Raney over Sterling McNeel "behind a door with Sterling McNeel." Dr. Samuel E. Asbury to Harriet E. Smither, October 2, 1945.

[24] Emeline Westall was a daughter of James Westall and a sister of Mrs. John Greenville McNeel. Eliza Westall Austin-Phillips married Colonel William G. Hill on February 25, 1836. Her son, Stephen,

very good looking and vain of her charms. She was a good girl fond of a romp. Her sister married Mr. G. McN. Emeline was about eighteen years old, quite a pleasant girl. I had met her at the town of Brazoria often before and at many balls and parties. She had been the Belle of the country before our arrival, and, it was said, quite a favorite of Mr. S. McN. She got into a play with me, and as I was still weak in the lack of strength, I begged her to desist. She replied, "I intend to whip you, Miss R, for taking my beau from me, and I wish you had stayed at Brazoria and not come into our neighborhood." I was nearly exhausted when at last I succeeded in throwing her down, and I sat on her person and paid her up in her own coin by tickling her. She cried, "Let me up, Old England, and I will never trouble you any more." I said, "Will you acknowledge you are whipped?" "Yes, yes," she cried, "I am whipped by old England." At this moment, whilst we still lay on the floor, and I still sitting on the top of her body, in came Mr. Munson and Mr. S. McN from behind a door in another room, laughing heartily at us both and having overheard all that passed between us and had seen us fighting. I felt ashamed and left the

---

was living with his grandmother, Mrs. Thomas Westall, while going to school to Thomas J. Pilgrim on Gulf Prairie.

The Thomas Westall plantation joined James Westall's, yet the cholera seems to have done no harm at Mrs. Thomas Westall's. Emeline, living at the James Westall place, was one of its victims. Her corpse, with several others there, remained unburied because neighbors were afraid to enter the plantation. *Ibid.*

room to recover my breath which was nearly exhausted. Emeline now ran out of the room also.

A week longer stay with my benefactors and I at last, by much persuasion, got her permission to make a visit to Mrs. C[25] in Brazoria. Had she known my intentions never to return, she would not have been willing to let me depart. It was not right that Mrs. R should be deprived of seeing her brother, who she thought much of, on my account. He was a great favorite in the family, and they called him Doctor as he generally doctored all the negroes on the plantation. They missed his visits more than she would acknowledge to me. My ancestral pride had returned. I was myself again. I was furnished with a horse, and a boy rode behind me to bring the horse back. A change of clothes was all I took with me to prevent suspicion.

We got along well until we came to the big pond of water, which was the same I passed in the night on my arrival at Mr. R's. I charged the boy to be careful and not touch the horse or whip him until we were across. About half way the horse began to plunge and rear up. He first kicked off the boy and then myself, then went out, leaving us both in the water. He then went in a lope for home. On recovering myself, for I went to the bottom of the pond, I saw the boy standing on shore shaking his wet locks of

[25] Dr. Jesse Counsel. An advertisement in *The Telegraph and Texas Register*, December 17, 1836, indicates that William Eckel of Brazoria desired to clear up the estate of the late Dr. Jesse Counsel.

hair. Whilst I was angry enough with him to have given him a whipping, if I could have reached him, but I had to look to my own safety, for I got out of my depth, the water up to my neck, and was only held up by my riding skirt which was camel's hair and so thick no water could penetrate it. I was standing on top of the water, buoyed up by my skirt, like a ship in full sail. I saw a bush about three or four yards' distance from me. My object was to reach this and hold on until I cold take another plunge, then I should not be far from getting out. This I did, going to the bottom a second time. On rising, I caught a twig of the bush and supported myself until I recovered my breath, which was gone for a minute. Whilst under the water for a minute I was touching the bottom of the pond with my feet, and lifting my riding skirt a little out of the way, I waded out, falling down several times before I got footing on land.

The boy stood strembling, fearing I would punish him. After scolding him good, I left the whipping to be done by his master, knowing that he would be sure to get one from Mr. R. I divested myself of my riding skirt and bonnet, and we took the road for home. The boy said he did not do anything to the horse that he knew of. "Only," said he, "I might have touched him with my feet in the flanks, and that will cause him to rear up every time." Mrs. R, seeing the horse return without a rider, suspected all was not right and immediately sent Mr. R in pursuit of us, he taking the road we left home on, but as we did not return the same way, we missed him, who did not return until noon. On returning home I found Mrs. R waiting with the anxiety of a parent. On seeing me, she said, "What has happened, Miss Ann?" "Why, Mr. S's horse has shown me his heels and has thrown me and your boy off in the big pond, and it was a great difficulty for me to get out without being drowned. I believe your boy was the cause, as he hit the horse in the flanks, which he says he will not stand without rearing up." On being questioned by his master, he denied hitting the horse. Nevertheless, he got a whipping that night from his master. Next day I started again, Mr. R going with me until I crossed the pond. On parting, he said, "I will send for you in a week, Miss Ann." I said, "very well."

On my arrival at Dr. Counsel's they were glad to see me. In a few days after my arrival at the town of B there was a ball at Mrs. L's. Many invitations were sent out into the country. I did not wish to attend, as my father and mother had been dead but a few months. But being overruled by my friends I went reluctantly. My dress was a white swiss muslin trimmed with black crepe, trimming of a handsome quality, and was said to be very becoming.

Mrs. L was a lady of dignified manners, and a favorite on account of being an old settler. Her hubsand was killed by Indians,[26] and she escaped by her fortitude and

[26] Dr. James Long was the last of the Texas filibusters. His ill-fated attempt to establish a republic resulted in his surrendering to the Mexicans, and he was shot on April 8, 1842, while in Mexico pleading his case to Agustín de Iturbide. W. Eugene Hollon and Ruth Lapham Butler (eds.), *William Bollaert's Texas*, fig. 8, 159–60.

bravery. She was about forty at this time, had a beautiful daughter who was married, although she was very young, I think not more than eighteen. Her husband died very shortly after our arrival in the country with consumption. My sister and self were great favorites with Mrs. L and her daughter. On the death of my mother, Mrs. L and Mrs. Anderson attended her until her last breath was gone. She took my sister home with her, where she remained until she was well enough to go to Captain Chase's at Velasco, whose lady was very anxious to have my sister live with her, having taken quite a fancy to her.

Doctor C was concocting a plan to give a ball at his house. Mrs. C and self were busily occupied shopping for the occasion. After being at Mrs. C's one week, my kind friend Mrs. R sent a boy with a horse for me to return on, but I would not see the boy who came for me and got Mrs. C to plead my excuse by saying she could not spare me so soon, that I must remain sometime longer with her. Mrs. R did not send after me any more, and I was glad of it, as I did not wish to return. Mr. S. McN was independent of his father; he worked twenty hands on his father's plantation and was in business with a Mr. Woodson[27] in the town of Brazoria in a dry goods store. I met with him in the town of B several times, and he was as attentive as ever. At balls and parties also he danced with

[27] This could have been Francis D. Woodson, who, as a member of the Santa Fe Expedition in 1842, was killed by Indians in Palo Duro. *The Telegraph and Texas Register*, August 3, 1842. John Henry Brown lists a James W. Woodson as serving in Brown's company in the Battle of Velasco, but there is no evidence to connect him with McNeel nor with merchandising.

no other young lady but myself, but often with married ladies. He did not come to see me at Dr. C's, but when invited to the ball he came. In dancing with me during the night, he observed, "I have heard, Miss Ann, you are going to be married." "To whom," I replied, "To whom?" "To Mr. John T of Caney." "This is not so, Mr. McN. Mr. T has been at the house several times; I suppose this is how the report originated." "If I thought you were going to get a man who would make you happy, I would not mind so much, but I do not think he will." I answered, "I have never thought of such a thing once." "Has he never paid you any attention?" "Yes he has, but he has never spoken to me on the subject of marriage." He then said, "I love you like a brother, Miss Ann, and I would kill the man who ever dares to mistreat you." At this moment someone interrupted our conversation. I was called to take my place in the dance. At twelve o'clock at night we retired to the supper room, which everyone said was tastifully arranged by my own hands, with evergreens and flowers. The supper table was also much admired. "Is it not beautiful?" cried several voices at once. "I wonder who set the supper table?" "It is the handsomest table set I have ever seen." "I expect Miss R had a hand in it." "Mrs. C will tell us." They all did honors to the table, pronounced everything delicious upon it. I had been a week in arranging things for it. I had robbed all the flowers gardens in town to dress the table with, and on hearing myself complimented by everyone for my taste, I was amply repaid for my labour and trouble.

Third Book

One or two weeks previous to the ball, I saw a gentleman coming down the street and go into the billiard room on the opposite side of the street. I asked Mrs. C if she knew him. She replied she did not. "I think it is some stranger just come into town as he has his riding whip in his hand. I should not be in danger of falling in love with him. She asked why. I replied he was too consequential. In one hour afterwards, the Doctor came home and said, "Miss Ann, I wish you to put on your best attire this evening. I am going to bring home a beau for you. He is a rich bachelor and wishes to get married very much. You must set your cap for him; he will be a good husband for you." I laughed and told him I believed he was getting tired of me and wished to get rid of me by marrying me off to some old bachelor. "Not so, Miss R." he said, "unless you could do well for yourself; and I know you would if you should get Mr. T. He is a man well known in the country, out of debt, and has a good home to take a wife to."

That evening after supper he came, and to my surprise, I found him the same little consequential fop I saw going into the billiard room in the morning. Mr. T was a man about thirty years of age, black hair and eyes, good complexion, good looking, and a good address, a pleasant smile upon his features, and very communicative. He had one of his arms broken which turned a little out of its natural position. This gave his arm a swagger that I took for conceit of his own personal dignity. A game of whist was proposed; we went to play one, but were soon compelled to quit as Mr. T was not sufficiently acquainted with the game to play.

I retired to the other end of the room to get my sewing. The Doctor and Mrs. C left the room for a short time, which seemed a long time to me. Mr. T drew his chair up to the table where I sat and commenced the following conversation. "I think I have been introduced to you before, Miss R, about six months ago at Mr. B's,[1] who kept the ferry across the river B. I was crossing a yoke of oxen. Do you remember me? Captain B was with you, and I understood from Mr. B that you were to be married to Captain B." I told him I recollected the time. "I see you are not married yet, Miss R." "No, sir," I replied, "It isn't quite soon enough for that event." He then remarked, "How do you like this country, Miss R?" I replied, "I like it well enough, but we have been very unfortunate in losing our parents in a foreign land, without relations or home." "As far as a home is concerned,"

[1] Bell's Landing was founded by Josiah H. Bell and laid out in 1824. The settlement grew into Marion and later into East Columbia. Webb, *The Handbook of Texas*, I, 533.

47

he replied, "Miss R, I think I can offer as good a one as any man in the country, if you will accept it. I am not like a terrapin that carries all upon my back. I have plenty at home to make you comfortable. I know you have a great many suitors who can make many flattering speeches to you, which I cannot. I am plain as a book."

This speech brought the color to my face, and I would have given anything to have left the room. He, seeing me silent, proceeded by saying, "I live thirty miles from here and the water courses are difficult to pass. If I come often to Brazoria, I shall make no crop, as I have no overseer. I should like, Miss R, if you could let me know if it is worth my while to come and see you again and pay my respects to you. I expect to leave town tomorrow morning, but will come back and see you again before I leave."

Before we had finished breakfast next morning, in walked Mr. T. I was again caught for another day's courtship. I tried to excuse myself by saying I had to go and meet a friend, but he would not let me off and made himself as agreeable as possible. When evening came I could hardly believe I had been sitting all day in his company. Next day I was in hopes he would go home, but I was disappointed. He stayed this day also. He had been three days in town, notwithstanding he came in such a hurry and said he must leave the next day. He had appointed to return in one week from the time he left. I thought I would be absent, but he came in before breakfast and left

me no chance to escape. It was during those visits he had
been seen by Mr. McN coming to the house. Now Mr. T
had proposed marriage to me and waited my answer.

After many a debate in my own mind I determined
to accept of Mr. T's proposal. He had visited me about
half a dozen times; he was well known in the country;
everyone spoke well of him. This was satisfactory to me.
He had given me several references as to his standing as
a man in society.

It was on returning from seeing [a friend] and his
family one evening, I was called in the street by someone.
On looking around I saw Mrs. S[2] who was now keeping
the same hotel as Mrs. L used to keep, Mrs. L having
retired into private life with her daughter into the country. Mrs. S said, "I wish to see you a little while." I went
in, took off my bonnet when Mrs. S remarked, "I hear

---

[2] Meriweather Woodson Smith purchased the tavern belonging
to Mrs. Jane Long. Muir, *Texas in 1837*, 186ff. On March 23, 1834,
William Barrett Travis wrote in his diary that Mrs. Long had sold her
boarding house at Brazoria, but in 1837 she opened a hotel at Richmond. Webb, *The Handbook of Texas*, II, 76. The *Brazoria Advocate*
of March 27, 1834, contained this notice:

Mrs. Jane H. Long takes this method of returning her un-
feigned thanks to the citizens of Brazoria and vicinity for the
very liberal patronage bestowed on her during her two years of
keeping a public house . . . and informs them she has retired from
business. . . . Mr. M. W. Smith, having purchased the entire
concern and being aided by Mr. and Mrs. Stephenson, she has
no hesitation in recommending them to the public.

you are going to be married to Mr. T." "Who told you so" I replied. "Mr. T himself." "He is rather too communicative," I said. She replied, "You need not be ashamed of him. He is one of the finest men in the country. He will make you a good husband." She then went on to tell all his good qualities and said nothing about the bad ones. I came out of her house to go home when I was met by Mrs. A, another friend of Mr. T and one of mine also. She got hold of my arm and said, "Come take a walk with me up the street." I complied. She commenced with, "I hear you are going to be married to Mr. T. Is it so?" I was silent. "If you marry him you will get a close stingy husband; and he has got a woman at home, one of his servants that will turn you out of doors before you have been home one month. He has lived a bachelor so long, he knows every grain of coffee that goes into his pot."

I listened patiently to this unpleasant news and said little in return. We did not stay long; or rather, I made my walk as short as possible without seeming rude, and bid her good evening. I was determined to tell Mr. T of what his friend Mrs. A had said the next time we met, for he was a constant visitor at their house. I was looking for him to come in town daily. Had my death knell going to be sounded, I could not have dreaded it any more. I was trying to summon up all my fortitude for the occasion when in walked Mr. T. He came up to myself first and shook my hand and then passed on to the rest of the family. As soon as breakfast was finished Mr. T and myself were left alone in the breakfast room.

He first broke the silence by saying, "I hope, Miss Ann, you have made up your mind to make me happy. It is to receive your answer I came to town today. I came near getting drowned crossing Linnville's Bayou,[3] but I shall be repaid for the dangers I have passed if you consent to be my wife." My silence seemed to give consent, and he took my hand in his and pressed it warmly, while I burst into an agony of tears. "You shall never have cause to repent being my wife. I will do everything in my power to make you happy." I now told him what his friend Mrs. A had said. He seemed surprised and said, "Everyone is jealous of my expected happiness. You may pay no attention to anything you may hear against me. If you do not find strict obedience from every servant I have got, I will sell the first one that dares to insult or disobey you. I have a woman called Minerva who I raised from a child. She is a smart field hand and in cotton picking time she picks 300 pound a day. In my absence she is my overseer, and though she is sometimes saucy she knows better than to give my wife any insolence." I told him I should expect perfect obedience from everyone of his servants, and should they prove otherwise, he must sell them, which he said he would do. I told him I wished my sister to live with us. He said it would give him great pleasure to offer her a home.

[3] Linnville Bayou, which rises in western Brazoria County, flows southeast seventeen miles along the Brazoria-Matagorda county line, draining into Caney Creek in southeastern Matagorda County. Webb, *The Handbook of Texas*, II, 61.

He then went into town to make arrangements for our wedding. He was determined that no expense should be spared to make a handsome supper, which was to be provided at the hotel, Doctor C's house not being large enough to entertain all that were invited. Mr. T left for home next day, and a week from that day was the one appointed for our wedding day. Mr. T gave me an order on Mr. M's store to get anything I wanted for the occasion. I was now busy as a bee making up my wedding suit, which was of rich white satin with blond lace, white silver artificial flowers, silver tinsel belt, black kid shoes with white satin rosettes and a gold bracelet, gold chain and no veil. This was all of my wedding dress. I had been in a fever of excitement all week, and with no appetite.

The day arrived. It rained in the morning so hard the streets were one sheet of water. Mr. T arrived early in the morning bringing the girl Minerva, who I understood was such a high minded piece of humanity. He brought a boy to wait upon himself. At three o'clock in the evening I left Dr. C's house for the hotel on horse back with Mr. T. The streets were very muddy from the recent rain. The sun shone out with all its brightness. There was a possibility that before night the water would dry up sufficiently to admit of our visitors to attend our marriage. The amphibious race, the frogs, were silenced by the subduing melody of the winged tribes; all nature was bespangled with smiles. I alone seemed sad. Everyone else seemed cheerful. My intended tried to cheer me, as he saw me look thoughtful, and never left my side only when obliged to. We had a private room to ourselves, and when it was time to dress he left me and went to dress also. Crowds of persons began to flock in from the country, and by seven o'clock in the evening the hotel was filled to overflowing by two hundred persons.

Ours was the first public wedding given at the town of Brazoria. At eight o'clock my bridesmaids arrived, one a Miss Anderson,[4] the other a Miss Bailey[5] with whom we found my father on our arrival in Texas. Mr. T had two groomsmen, one Mr. Edmond St. J. Hawkins, the other a gentleman whose name I have forgotten.[6] At eight

---

[4] The bridesmaid probably was a daughter of Simeon Asa Anderson, one of Stephen F. Austin's Old Three Hundred, who received title to one league of land in present Fayette County on August 10, 1824, and who was listed in the census of Austin's colony, 1826, as a farmer and stock raiser, aged twenty-five to forty, and the father of a son and two daughters.

[5] James Briton Bailey had at least five daughters: Sarah, Margaret, Nancy, Betsy, and Pollie. On another page of her journal, Ann mentions Sally Bailey, and it is probable that it was she who served as the bridesmaid.

[6] Two early editions of *The Telegraph and Texas Register* mention Edmund St. John Hawkins. On May 30, 1837, the newspaper printed an advertisement signed by George N. Hawkins, administrator, notifying persons not to "trespass or waste" upon the lands "of the late Edward [*sic*] St. John Hawkins, deceased," and a second notice, published September 2, 1837, and signed by Littleberry Hawkins of Brazoria, urged all persons having claims against the estate of the late Edmund St. John Hawkins to present them within the legally prescribed time in order to have them honored. The name of Edmund St. John Hawkins also is included on the roll of Texans participating in the Battle of Velasco.

The marriage bond of Ann Raney and John Thomas, signed

o'clock we entered the ball room to be married, it being the
largest room in the house. The bridesmaids and groomsmen went first into the room, myself and Mr. T last. I felt
much abashed at the presence of so many people, and my
eyes which on first entering had been cast to the ground
were now raised to the face of Mr. Smith, the presiding alcalde,[7] who was going to perform the marriage ceremony.
A breathless silence pervaded the room whilst the ceremony was performed. The alcalde himself was so much
excited that he paused once or twice whilst performing the
ritual. I looked at the bridesmaids who were tastefully
dressed. They looked like marble statues. As for myself,
I trembled from head to foot, and when the ceremony
was finished and the alcalde told Mr. T to salute his bride,
I saw no motion made by him to do it. At last, feeling for
his embarrassment, I turned my cheek to his so that he
might more easily salute me, which he did. The same was
done by the bridesmaids and groomsmen, the groomsmen

February 14, 1833, by Henry Smith, alcalde, was witnessed by E. St.
John Hawkins and W. H. Settle.

[7] As part of the State of Coahuila and Texas, Texas was divided
into departments of Nacogdoches, Bexar, and Brazos, and subdivided
into municipalities or jurisdictions, over each of which presided an
alcalde. On July 24, 1834, Henry Smith was notified of his appoint-
ment as Political Chief of the Department of Brazos by Viesca, the
Mexican governor. The commission came through the hands of William Barrett Travis, secretary of the Ayuntamiento of San Felipe, who
wrote: "Allow me to congratulate you as the first American who has
been appointed to the office of Political Chief, and to hope that you may
be the mean of great good to Texas." John Henry Brown, *The Life of
Henry Smith*, 16–25.

kissing me first, then the bridesmaids. We then went out as we came in until tea and coffee were ready. Then we all assembled in the dining room where tea, coffee and cakes were handed around.

I saw a multitude of people, half of whom I was unacquainted with. The ladies were dressed very gay and in good taste and might have vied with city belles. After tea our congratulations commenced. I stood up with my husband until I was nearly exhausted, receiving one after another. At last a chair was brought me, and I sat down and only rose when obliged to. The dance had commenced and not more than half of the company had been presented to us. About ten o'clock that night I got liberty to dance for a short time. My engagements were too many to fill, so I danced but little that I might give offense to none. About twelve o'clock at night supper was announced by our hostess, Mrs. S, and we retired to the supper room. Everything was tastefully arranged and the table laden with every delicacy that could be procured. Fruit from Orleans was in abundance, the cake delicious, fowl and meats plentiful, plenty of wine, also coffee. All eyes were on my husband and myself, so I ate but little; a cup of coffee was grateful to me, as it had always been my favorite beverage.

I hurried to retire where I would not be so closely observed. Everyone praised my dress, which I made myself, and said I looked charming but sad. This was a truth. I masked the feeling of my heart on this night that I might make him who I had chosen for my husband feel happy. At one o'clock I went up to my room with my servant Minerva, who, I had forgotten to state, was all obedience. I dismissed her shortly afterwards and I was left alone. My bridesmaids insisted on waiting upon me to disrobe me and see me in bed, but I would not permit them to and told them to go and enjoy themselves in the ball room. I had been sitting in one position half an hour before a looking glass that reflected my form to my view, when I thought, "I am dressed and adorned for a sacrifice." I had been sitting in one position without a motion to undress. My thoughts were on my native land with my dear brother and Henry, who I never expected to forget; my love was still his, and parted only by force of circumstances. I was disappointed in not seeing that beloved face, my sister, at my wedding.

In the midst of these reflections, someone opened the door and the alcalde put in his head. "My dear, are you not in bed? Your husband wishes to retire for the night, and it is my business, according to the Spanish law, to see you both in bed."[8] I felt indignant to this method of

[8] In his thesis, "The History of Fort Bend County," 79, J. L. Bridges writes:

> Another aim of the Mexican government was to convert the colonists to their Catholic belief. The priest designated to this domain made periodic visits during which he performed marriages that had been consummated by *alcaldes*, and christened children long since born. When married by the *alcaldes*, the bride and groom had to sign a bond promising to have the holy rites performed during the next visit of the priest.

Noah Smithwick, in *The Evolution of a State*, gives details of the

the Spanish law and promised to go to bed directly. With this promise he closed the door. My face, if anyone could have seen it, was crimson with blushes. And my husband came in and I was still sitting there with all my clothes on. He was surprised at seeing me still up, and taking my hand and kissing it, he said, "My child, I will be a father as well as a husband. Do not sit there, but go to ged and take some rest, for you have need of it. Tomorrow you have a long and tiresome journey to take. The roads are bad, and without rest, you will be unfit for it. I want to start as soon as we get breakfast."

I hid my face in my handkerchief and wept bitter tears. Would he fulfill all he had promised? I had need of a father's and a husband's care. I was fifteen years younger than Mr. T and a child in appearance to himself. Without saying any more he went to the other end of the room, my back being turned to him, and in a few minutes he was in bed. On turning around, I found him gone to bed. I slipped off my dress and all my ornaments, blew out the light, and in a few minutes I was also in bed. Shortly afterwards in came my evil genius with a light in his hand, opened a part of the bar and looked at us both the space of a minute and was gone without speaking. My husband laughed and so did I, though no one saw me do so for I hid my face with the cover.

arrangement in explaining the wedding of a Miss Cartwright to Nicholas McNutt. "The alcalde tied the nuptial knot in good American style but the contracting parties had in addition to sign a bond to avail themselves of the priest's services to legalize the wedding at the earliest opportunity."

Mr. T was up before day, and Mrs. S and many of the gentlemen who had never gone to bed went to the horse lot to joke him for being up so early, and he wished himself away from Brazoria and in his quiet home. In an hour from the time he got up, breakfast was ready. I was in hopes it was too early for anyone to be up, only those laid down, but when I went to the table it was crowded. As breakfast was over, I put on my riding skirt, which was the same one I had when thrown from Mr. S. McN's horse in the pond. I had a black silk basque, green broadcloth riding cap, with a plume of black ostrich feathers, white satin rosette on one side. A great many bouquets hung in a small basket on the horn of my saddle presented me by my friends. When ready to start, everyone grasped my hand to bid me adieu until it was sore from shaking hands with so many friends. On leaving the hotel three cheers went up for us, and three more for the Caney boys, in compliment to Mr. T's taking the only Belle in Brazos.

I had a nice pony of iron gray bought by Mr. T expressly for me, and a natural pacer. We found the roads bad, and it was night before we reached Mr. H's on Cedar Creek or Lake.[9] They were old people, had one son, who like the Dutchman's pig, little but old. We were enter-

[9] James Hensley was in Stephen F. Austin's colony in April, 1824, and received title to one *sitio* and one labor of land in present Brazoria and Austin counties. Although he was not listed in the census of the colony for 1836, John Hensley, J. M. Hensley, and H. Hensley were. William Barrett Travis noted the death of "Old Hensley" in his diary on May 4, 1834, without indicating which member of the family he meant. Webb, *The Handbook of Texas*, I, 799.

tained kindly, and as were tired, went to bed early. After supper, Mrs. S had put no small quantity of cake and other nice things for our lunch on the road. I slept from fatigue, the first sleep that did me any good in a week.

In the morning, we started early again. It was but thirty miles, but the roads being so bad, it took us two days to reach home. I inquired many times of Mr. T if this or that place was his, being impatient to arrive at home. He replied, "No, but we will soon reach there now. We are but a few miles from my plantation." Presently we came to Caney Creek, which seemed full of water. After stopping a few minutes on the brink, Mr. T observed to me, "I think Caney is swimming, but don't be afraid. It is not far across. Follow me; it has a hard bottom. There is no danger of our horses bogging down." I looked after as he went into the creek with his horse, frequently saw him swimming with him. I felt afraid and told him so. After some encouraging words from him, I whipped my horse into the creek. I was soon wet over the knees, my horse swimming but a short distance. The banks of the creek were steep and our horses found difficulty in getting up them. We were now on the opposite bank. On looking up I saw a little log cabin, a beautiful orchard of peach trees, a fine vegetable garden and lawn in front of the house. "Whose place is this?" "This is my place," said Mr. T. "How glad I am," I replied. "I have got home."

On entering the enclosure, a nice, tidy mulatto woman met us at the door. She helped me off my horse and said with a polite curtsy, "I am glad, Mr., you have come home." I went into the house and as I was entering the passage through the middle of the cabin, I hit my head against the roof. I remarked to Mr. T, "I think you will have to raise the roof of your house or build a new one" "Oh, my child," he replied, "I had no one to fix for when I built this house. Now I have got a wife, I will build a better one." Every place was the essence of cleanness, and although a puncheon floor, it was clean enough to eat off. The furniture was all hand made, chairs with deerskin bottoms, tables and bedstead fixtures. Dinner was prepared and we, being hungry, did honor to the table, which was filled with vegetables of all kinds, milk and butter, and the best kind of corn bread. At this time I was not very fond of corn bread, which my husband observing, asked me if I liked it. On replying I was not fond of it, he said he would get some flour for me shortly. "At present we are out."

After dinner he asked me to take a walk with him in the field, "where my negroes are at work. I want to see how they have got along in my absence." On coming near enough for the hands to see us, they cheered us once or twice, and when they came up to us each one congratulated us on our happiness with a shake of the hand. They all appeared glad to see us, and Mr. T was satisfied with the work they had done in his absence.

The first thing I thought of was to send after my sister, who had not been able to attend my marriage on account of ill health, having chills and fever all the time, or every other day. Two weeks after I was married, I sent my pony for her, and in four days after I sent for her, she was landed at my own log cabin. Tears of joy filled both our eyes on meeting, as we had been separated two or three months. My sister was delighted with everything she saw, and especially with my husband, with whom she was a great favorite. She said she felt at home once more. She busied herself about everything, and was in truth able to do nothing. Her health recovered from change of air and diet. She was fond of milk and we had plenty of it. In a few weeks she got fat as a pig in its pen.

About two weeks after we were married, Mr. Colonel Williams[10] gave us an infare dinner and ball at night, which was well attended. Mr. W was a widower at this time and was paying attention to a lady, Miss W, called the Navidad Belle.[11] She was a handsome girl, black hair and black eyes, her complexion fair as an alabaster doll. It was at Mr. W's house I was introduced to her for the

[10] This could refer to George I. Williams, one of the Old Three Hundred who was listed in the census of 1836 as a farmer and stock raiser, aged between twenty-five and forty, married, and with three sons and two daughters. The census of January, 1837, does not mention his wife. He attended a meeting of colonists protesting against the Fredonian Rebellion and declaring loyalty to Mexico. *Ibid.*, II, 911.

[11] The term "Navidad Belle" should not be confused with the popular legend of the "wild woman of the Navidad" which circulated between 1837 and 1850 and which received wide newspaper publicity. The legend is narrated by Martin M. Kennedy in *Legends of Texas*, (242–53), a publication of the Texas Folklore Society edited in 1924 by J. Frank Dobie. Ann Raney probably refers to the daughter of Samuel Addison White, who lived on the Navidad River and who served in the marine company under Captain William J. Russell in the Battle of Velasco.

first time. I found her a very agreeable lady, and we enjoyed ourselves much. We only broke up dancing at daylight. We were provided a good dinner and a better supper. Mr. W in three weeks afterwards was married to Miss White of the Navidad River.[12] He said he could not resist the example set for him by Mr. T and Mr. J who were both his neighbors and recently married. Mrs. W was a kind neighbor and a sincere friend. We were both young and good company for each other.

I was surprised one day about six months after our marriage by a call from a Major H,[13] a man about sixty, who was six foot high, good looking, fair hair and eyes. He was a friend of my husband's, and visited us sometimes, not often, lived about nine miles from us. He wished a private interview. I was wondering what he would have to say to me. On going out of the house, he said, "I have come to get your consent to marry your sister, you being her only relation living, and could wish to have your sanction." I was surprised at this information. "When and where did you do your courting?" "At your

[12] The Navidad River rises in the southern part of Fayette County and forms East, Middle and West Forks which unite in Lavaca County. The name is a Spanish word meaning birth. Webb, *The Handbook of Texas*, II, 264.

[13] Witnessed April 10, 1834, by Robert H. Williams and John Thomas and filed April 22, 1834, by Edwin Waller, alcalde, the marriage bond of Samuel Hoit and Mary Raney agreed that "if the said Samuel and Mary should rather on application from the other refuse to have their union legally solemnized than the other shall or may sue the other for the full and lawful sum of $5,000. . . ."

house, Madam," he replied. He had been to our house several times, but I never saw anything in his manners that could have made me think he ever dreamed of paying attention to my sister. One day they both went into the peach orchard to get peaches. This was the only time I could remember seeing them together alone. At last I said, "Major, I have a serious objection to your years. I suppose you are in circumstances good enough to take care of a wife. If my sister can be happy with you, she is old enough to judge for herself." Here our conversation was brought to a close.

After his departure I questioned my sister about her strange choice, asked her if she really loved him, and if she was in earnest about marrying him, a man old enough for her grandfather. She said, "I cannot say I love Major H, but should he treat me kindly, I can make him happy." "You cannot be happy with a man so much older than yourself, a strange choice for a girl of seventeen." My sister was very whimsical about many things and I now thought her more so than ever. She was very intelligent, and interesting with a fine intellect, and good enough in my estimation for a prince. To think of her nursing an old superannuated man, whilst there were so many young men her own age who would have been glad to call her wife! After frequent expostulations with her on the subject, and finding all my advice to no effect, the wedding day was appointed, which took place early one morning first of the fall months. A few of the neighbors were invited and in one hour afterwards they started for home.

Mrs. W and myself continued to visit and were like sisters in friendship. One day Mrs. Atkinson came to visit me and spent the day. I promised to return home with her in the evening and stay all night with her as my husband had gone to Brazoria. On going home with her in the evening and coming to a turn in the road, we heard a noise like the grunting of hogs. On hearing them Mrs. A said, "What if they should be Mexican hogs?"[14] "Oh no," I said, "I think they are some of ours or our neighbor's hogs. There are no Mexican hogs about at present." "Yes, but there are," replied she, "my husband saw a drove of them somewhere about here."

The words had hardly been spoken when we came up on seven of them. Mrs. A on seeing them said, "Run! Run, Mrs. T. They are Mexican hogs!" She left me standing in the road, hardened with unbelief. I had not yet noticed the difference between them and our tame hogs. Having stood about three minutes looking at them, I noticed how small and short their legs were, when presently one or two bristled up at me, gnashed their tusks which were very long and large, and came after me. I took to my heels and ran as fast as I could. Looking back, I saw my pursuers close at my heels. I doubled my speed, and soon passed my friend Mrs. A on the road She cried,

[14] "Mexican hog or peccary: These are found generally in the low hollows of trees and shot; the meat is very good." Hollon and Butler, *William Bollaert's Texas*, 263. Smithwick, writing in *The Evolution of a State* (26), commented that "Old Man Varner had a lot of wild hogs running in the Brazos bottom lands on his place, and when he wanted pork, he simply went out and shot it."

"Oh, do not leave me, Mrs. T, or I shall faint in the road. I have run until I can run no longer." I told her I was going to the creek to get Mr. A to bring his gun to shoot the hogs, he being there with some three or four other men crossing some corn. She still cried after me, but I paid no attention to her cries, as I did not see the hogs anywhere, we having outrun them or either they got tired pursuing.

On arriving at the creek I was met by Mr. A in his shirt and drawers, with a sack of corn on his back, and one or two other men in like condition, some having their shirts off with their drawers on, which they were trying to put on when I got to the creek, our screams having attracted their attention, seeing us pass a short time before, were coming to our rescue. When I met them with their clothes in their hands, I told Mr. A that we had been followed by Mexican hogs and that his wife was on the road running for her life, and to make haste as she was nearly exhausted. It is hard to determine whether I was more alarmed at the Mexican hogs or the men in a state of nudity for they cut a singular figure. They had been carrying the corn across the creek in sacks, by hand, there being no boat and the creek low at this time.

I had not been long home when Mr. A arrived with his wife, but so exhausted from fatigue as to be unable to return home that night. Next day she was quite ill and a physician was sent for. He said her heart was injured by the fat melting over it. Mrs. A was very fleshy, weighed about two hundred and was only twenty years of age. She remained about three days at our house before she could be moved home. She told my husband there was a stump of a tree in the road about two feet high, and rather than take time to go around it, that I jumped over it. A considerable feat for me in my condition! Mrs. A recovered in time but was sick for several months afterwards. Mr. A was joked by the neighbors on his being half naked, also the men with him, when called to rescue us from the Mexican hogs.

It was peach time and we had a fine orchard full of fine ones. I was climbing on the fence one day to get some and was knocking them off with a long cane when I fell from the top of the fence to the ground. I soon jumped up as I did not wish anyone to see me, as my husband had often charged me not to get upon the fence to get peaches, as he was afraid of an accident of this kind. I kept my secret a day or two; the same night of the accident I was taken sick, out of one spasm into another. I continued this way several days. At last I told my husband about my fall—as I was afraid of the consequences. He was much shocked at this information. I recovered but it was several weeks before I was able to be about.

One morning as I was seated at my sewing, a boy arrived with a letter from my sister saying that she was very sick and wished me to come to see her immediately. She had been in bad health some time and pronounced by her husband in the last stages of liver complaint, as he had been her only physician. After consulting Mr. T a horse was provided, and I returned with the boy to go to see my sister. On arriving at Mr. H's I found my sister weak and worn to a shadow of her former self. She was a martyr to medicine and had no more symptoms of liver complaint than myself, who I know was free from this disease at this time.

Major H had set the day when an abscess in her liver would break and gave her to understand that he had no hopes of her life. He was half his time under the influence of liquor, and never let her get outside of his plantation unless he accompanied her. She was indeed dying of low spirits and despondency. She was free from disease but weakened from taking purgatives. I told her she must quit taking medicine. She replied her husband forced her to take it, and he would not let her have any nourishing food to eat. I remonstrated with Major H on his course of treatment, which he persisted he was right in. Having given my sister some advice on how to get along with her husband for the future, and after staying three days, I left for my house leaving Major H in no very good humor, having given my sister all she wanted to eat during my stay of good nourishing diet under which she improved, also throwing aside all his medicine, which satisfied my sister so well, and spent in relating her troubles. We made my sister retire to bed early as she had need of rest.

Next day Major H arrived in pursuit of his wife who he found at our house, walking in the orchard, their old courting place, although very different the scene. Instead of love there was discord, the strings that played so sweetly were forever shattered and no more to the sound would give a token. I heard him say, "If you return I will never more taste liquor." But she was firm as some mountain that can be dislodged only by some revolution of nature. He did not come to the house, but on receiving his final answer got upon his horse and rode off. My sister and myself looked after him for a last time, for none of us ever saw him afterwards. On finding my sister resolved no more to live with him, he drank to excess and in one month was a corpse. She received several letters from him begging her to return, saying that he would quit drinking. It is not probable he ever would, as it had been a confirmed habit for years.

Major H was a widower when my sister married him and had several children living at the time of his death. His Negroes and plantation was mortgaged to his oldest son Judge I for as much as they were worth. After his father's death he wrote my sister saying if she would return to Major H's plantation and live there she might have all she could make off the place, but nothing could induce her to accept of a living that she was not the owner of. She wrote Mr. I to send someone to take possession of the Major's property as she did not wish to return, thanking him for his offer. The Major had never told my sister that his property was mortgaged, and she thought it his own until his death when she received a letter from his son.

One evening in November I was taken sick and physician sent for; Mr. B. H[15]—found it to be the son of General Harrison of Ohio. He had just come into the country to practice medicine. On meeting my sister and conversing with her, he seemed pleased in her society, so he often gave us a call and became a confirmed lover of my sister, Mary.

Reports flew around during this time injurious to himself, which I told my sister to acquaint him with. One was that he drank too much liquor, and the other that he was an imposter, that he was no more General H's son than she was the Queen of England. After my sister told him the reports in circulation, he told her that for the satisfaction of her sister, he would write his father and

[15] Major Benjamin Harrison, son of President William Henry Harrison, was born at North Bend, Ohio, on September 8, 1806, and although a graduate in medicine, was more adventurer than physician. As a young man he was threatened with alcoholism and made a trip to the far Northwest with the French fur trader Charles Larpenteur in the hope of recovering from the habit. He came to Texas in 1834 and married Mary Raney a short time later. His first wife was Louise Bonnet. In Texas, Dr. Harrison became a man of mystery and intrigue following his capture by the Mexican general José Urrea in April, 1836. He was dispatched as an emissary of good will to the Texas colonists, and Urrea records in his diary that the mission was successful. Herman Ehrenberg, a close observer and writer, considered Harrison an imposter and declared that the mission to Texas was a failure. After his release by Urrea, Harrison returned to Ohio, where he died June 17, 1840. Webb, *The Handbook of Texas*, I, 779.

President Benjamin Harrison is quoted in *Forty Years a Fur Trader on the Upper Missouri, the Personal Narrative of Charles Larpenteur, 1833–1872*, edited by Elliott Coues, as saying that his uncle, Dr. Harrison, ". . . was of a wild and adventurous disposition. . . ." See also Dr. Pat Ireland Nixon, "Dr. Benjamin Harrison, Temporary Texan," *Journal of the History of Medicine and Allied Sciences*, Vol. I, No. 1.

let me know all about him. In a short time afterwards, I received a letter from General H himself, stating that he had been requested by his son to address a few lines to me for my satisfaction. His son B, he said, he had sent to Texas, throwing him on his own resources for support. He said he had been in the habit of drinking, and during those times had run him into debt, telling me all his imperfections and everything relating to him, winding up by saying, "If your sister sees proper to marry my son after my stating the truth, the latch of my door shall never be shut against them, and my house shall be their house; but I never will give my son a fortune as he has spent one already for me, but at my death, I will provide for his wife and children," concluding by saying, "If you and your husband ever come to Ohio," he would be glad to see us.

As soon as I received the letter, I begged my sister not to think of marrying Mr. B. H. She had already seen trouble on account of an intemperate husband, to reflect seriously on the subject and wait until he reformed, specifying a time of six months for this purpose. Mr. H agreed to our proposition. I had never seen him under the influence of liquor, although many of his friends had; nevertheless, he was quite sober when he came to see Mary. In about two weeks after our contract, one morning as I came out of my room, I was surprised to find my sister's room door open, it being earlier than she was in the habit of rising. I went in and found her trunk of clothes gone. I suspected all was not right. On asking the servant if she

had seen my sister, she said she had not. After breakfast one of our neighbors, Mr. C, called at our house and
said there had been a wedding that morning and asked me
if I could guess who it was. I said, "Is it not my sister?"
He replied that it was. I was not much surprised.

Mr. B. H was a fine looking man, fair hair and eyes,
stood six foot high, fine form, very intelligent, and a
perfect gentleman in manners and address. I know my
sister loved him, and I am sure he did her. They did not
return to our house, as they knew I would be very far
from approving of such a course as they had pursued.
Major H had not been dead but three months. Propriety
itself would have called for them to have waited longer.
They went to housekeeping, and shortly after their marriage received supplies of provisions from Mr. H's father.
They lived but three miles from me. My sister wrote to
me to come and see her, but I did not get a chance to go.
Mr. B. H came several times with a message from my
sister, but I treated him a little cool, as I did not think he
had treated me right in running off with my sister and
having a clandestine marriage.

I now had a little son about three weeks old, who
my husband named Edmond St. John Hawkins T, after
one of his groomsmen. One day after my sister's second
marriage, my husband came home all excited. He had sold
his place and some of his Negroes to a man by the name
of Russell for the sum of ten thousand dollars, which I
thought at the time was very little. He had reserved some
four or five of his Negroes for himself out of the bargain.

Minerva was one he kept, and sold Daphney, my cook and housekeeper. I remonstrated with him for this, as I had much rather he had sold Minerva, a woman I never liked and one I found insolent to a degree.

Part of Mrs. A's prophesy had come to pass. My husband had her to punish many times since our marriage for her insolence to me. One night, getting angry with her husband, one of Mr. W's hands, she struck him with an axe which nearly severed him in two and injured him so badly he was never able to work in the field any more. So, Mr. W took him for his carriage driver, my husband having all his doctor bills to pay and half of what he cost Mr. W, besides five hundred exacted of my husband by Mr. W, which he paid. I could not prevail with my husband to keep our cook. He said if he did so, it would make null and void the sale of his place, and Mr. Russell knew well the value of Daphney, and Mr. R's wife was young and inexperienced housekeeper. This was the reason he wanted her.

Preparations were made for us to leave Caney and go on to the Brazos River to live, my husband having bought the same place where Mr. Bailey used to live, and the same gentleman we found my father staying with when we first came to the country. His daughter was one of my bridesmaids. I must state that Mr. Bailey was much addicted to drinking spiritous liquors and was insane during these times. In one of his drinking fits, he set fire to all his out houses, barn and stables. His dwelling house was only preserved by the entreaties of a favorite daughter. On getting sober and finding the mischief he had done, he determined upon selling his place, which had been bought by two other gentlemen previous to my husband's purchasing it. Mr. W being the last gentleman who owned it, and it sold for a little less money every time, and when we got it, it was thought quite a bargain, being eleven hundred acres in the whole. Mr. W lived six months upon the place and sold it to Mr. T for several hundred dollars less than he gave for it.

After Mr. B sold his place, he went to Brazoria to open a hotel and lived but a short time. He made a will which was a singular one. He was buried standing upright with his face to the west, and his gun in his arms, ready for a march. This was done and he requested to be buried upon the place that formerly belonged to him, which was done, in a pecan grove close to the house.

After a week's preparation, we left Caney for the Brazos River. I was sorry I did not get the time to visit my sister before I left. I was told she was on a visit to Judge D when we left, who lived some distance from us. So I was obliged to be satisfied, thinking I would visit her when I got settled in my new home. I was found in tears one day by Mr. T. He asked me the cause. I told him I should not like to leave without bidding my sister goodbye. He tried to console me by saying he would send after her some day after we got settled at our new home.

On arriving there, everyone of us was tired and thirsty. I took a survey of the place, which had a wild and gloomy appearance, such as you often read of in enchanted places. The dwelling house was painted red, a kitchen smoke house and some outbuildings; a pecan orchard about a quarter of a mile long lead like an avenue up to the house, having to cross a big pond of water before entering the grove. This pond was sometimes deep enough to sail a boat. Wild ducks, turkeys, cranes and other wild fowl were plentiful at this pond most of the year. In the grove close to the house was the grave of Mr. B, the first occupant of the place. It was about as large around as a wash tub bottom.[16]

I often took a walk in the grove and visited this spot. A strange whim, I thought, but a much stranger man when I visited him and his family during his life-time. I would say, "How are you today, Mr. B?" "Oh, madam, I am in sack cloth and ashes." This was when he had been drinking to excess and was repenting. I often went to see them as they had been kind to my father when in bad

[16] See Second Book, footnote 15. The legend of "Bailey's Light" is told by Gloria Swanson in *Backwoods to Border* (144–45), published by the Texas Folklore Society in 1943:

. . . sometimes when the family would gather on the front porch after supper, a ball of fire would rise out of the ground and wander over the country. The men would saddle their horses and follow it. Sometimes they would ride all night long, and usually near daylight they would see it return to the spot from which it had risen and sink into the ground. The spot was the grave of an early Texas pioneer named Bailey, who at his own behest had been buried standing up with his musket at his side and a lantern and a flask of whiskey at his feet. Some say the light is the flashing of the powder in Bailey's gun as he goes hunting in the night. Others say it is the lantern he carried to guide him through the swamps.

health. They were much respected and their house was a stopping house for travellers. He had a great many good riding horses, and Miss Sally used often to come to the town of B to get me to go and spend a day or two with her. We were sometimes accompanied by Capt. W. B.

Mr. T was getting ready to plant his crop, everyone else was at work in the field a quarter of a mile from the house, and I was in the house with my little boy one morning when I was startled by a young Indian. He spoke to me, but I could not understand him. He gave me some deer meat. I had no money and tried to make him understand that I had no change to buy it. "No want nothing." I thanked him but did not like to take it for I thought my husband might not be pleased. He was dressed tastefully with a deerskin dress and leggings, and no small quantity of ornaments of every description about his form. Every day he would return with meat and game of some kind. My husband would offer him money for his meat and game, but he would not take it. We gave him something to eat, and that was all he would accept. He made me presents of baskets out of rushes, all shapes and sizes, and would not take any pay for them. I was a great favorite with him and sometimes felt a little afraid in his company when my husband was not at the house, there being only my cook, Malinda and myself at the house.

One day he brought his mother, a very old woman, and introduced her to me in his own language. She examined everything about the house and seemed pleased. After presenting them something to eat, she told me she had twelve daughters and that she was going to bring them all to see me. I told her I should like to see them. One evening about a week after she had been to see me she came with all her daughters and a good many small children of her daughters'. They spoke pleasantly but their own language, and on being invited in the house sat down upon the floor. My husband was from home and I did not expect him to return that night. I made the girl set the table and gave them all a good supper, but instead of sitting at the table to eat, they all sat on the floor, and instead of using their knives and forks, they took the victuals between their fingers, not using their plates even, and seemed to enjoy my surprise by laughing heartily. After supper they left for their camp, which was on Mr. T's land, well pleased with their entertainment, about a mile distant. I was glad to get rid of them by showing them all the civility in my house, as I was afraid of so many of them together. Some of them were not a little impertinent, taking some things without asking if they were useful to me.

On the return of my husband he made them remove their camp, giving their chief to understand they had become troublesome at our house. I did not see the young Indian quite so often. He came sometimes, always bringing me a supply of deer meat and game. He was about six foot high, fine form and handsome features. Some of the Indians were hostile towards us at this time, the country newly setting up, and I felt afraid to be left alone with my servant girl, Malinda, and no other protection.

The Mexicans were far more numerous than Americans. They often stayed all night with us when traveling, and I learned enough of this language as to understand what they said.

My husband bought me a little Negro girl about six years old for a nurse for my boy. I was very glad of this as I found her very handy about the house. Sometimes she was disobedient and did not mind what I said to her, then I would threaten to whip her. Presently afterwards she was missing, and I would have to nurse myself that day. In the evening she would have to be brought home by some of the field hands, having found her hiding in some woods in the field. She got a whipping from my husband on the first sight of her. She often did the same thing, and caused me to get a scolding from Mr. T because he thought I threatened her too much without executing.

Cotton picking time arrived and my nurse was put into the fields to pick cotton. She picked 50 weight a day, and whenever she got tired she only waited for me to scold her a little and then ran away for the whole day. I then got scolded sure enough, as my husband did not like to lose his cotton; and rather than see him look a little out of temper at me about it, I went into the field myself and stayed until I thought I had her 50 weight. At night a search would be made for Adeline. When found she caught another whipping, but did not mind it only while she was getting punished. I often had to do her day's work and it provoked me not a little.

One day a gentleman stopped at our house. The

day being warm he called for water. Adeline was sent after it, but as she did not return my husband began to think she had fallen into the cistern, as we used to draw the water from the well by means of a rope and ladder. As she could not be found my husband got his men to go into the cistern to hunt for her, thinking sure she was drowned. On the men going into cistern they found the pitcher at the bottom with the hand broken off. On searching intently nothing was found of Adeline, so she must have run off this time also. She had broken the handle off the pitcher and was afraid to return. Nothing of her was seen that day, and not until before day next morning one of the men went to look for something he wanted under the dwelling house, where he found Adeline in a hole fast asleep. He caught her and brought her to the house, and my husband gave her a remembrance that time she did not soon forget. I was getting very tired of filling her place in the field, and when she asked me to beg her off from getting whipped, I replied, "No, Adeline, I begged you off for the last time." As I often used to go her security for better behavior, I was worn out with her running away and often wished I had never seen her. She was good to my little boy, but when she was obliged to work she was good for nothing. My husband was often out of humor with me on her account.

He was of a sullen temper, and if he did not say anything his looks were sufficient. I could soon tell when anything went wrong in the fields amongst his hands; he spoke but little. When in good humor, he told me not to mind him at such times, that he was not displeased with me. My husband had employed an overseer to help him by the name of George Paine.[17]

One morning my husband left home on business and told me he would not return for a week. Some three days after he was gone, after going to bed at night, the clock struck eleven. I was startled at someone walking in my room, with light shoes on. I spoke to Malinda who was sleeping in the room with me, in another bed. I called; she did not answer. I called again; still she was silent. I lay in my bed, the perspiration standing in big drops upon my forehead. I made an effort to rise, but it was fruitless. I was held back as with an iron chain. I had seen a face I knew, a stranger (Phoneme). I knew he was dead which made me more afraid. I lay still as death until morning. After seeing the face, I heard no more noise in the room.

It was a long night to me. At daylight, I woke Malinda. "Why did you not answer me last night when I spoke to you?" "I was afraid, for the spirits were walking here last night in our room. Did you not hear?" "Yes," I replied, without saying what I saw. On hearing footsteps she was too afraid to speak. "Now, Mrs., I will tell you what the folks say. This place is haunted by Mr. B and

[17] Listed among the thirty-two unattached members of Colonel J. W. Fannin's company at Goliad by Vernon Blake, *Goliad*, 42, is George Pain. The same spelling is given on page 52 of *History of Goliad* by Irene Hohmann Friedrichs. Brown, in his *History of Texas*, I, 602, indicates that George Paine, who fell in the massacre of Fannin's men, was one of the sixteen of Captain Albert C. Horton's troops who remained with Fannin while the other thirty-six retreated.

our men cannot milk the cows at night, for he is there and troubles them so much they can scarcely milk the cows at all. Jim cannot go home at night to see his wife, but he meets his master in the road and he will not let him pass." Jim was one of Mr. B's servants and was hired to us for the year, and was at this time owned by Mr. B's daughter who lived about a mile from us. Jim was always permitted to go to see his wife before the sunset. This I had noticed, but did not know the reason. My husband had forbid the servants to tell me the report that the place was haunted, as he knew I would not like to live there.

The next day I removed my bed clothes into the other room, the bedstead being a fixture to the house and the identical one Mr. B used to sleep in before he sold his place. Mr. Paine, our overseer, slept in the gallery under a pair of stairs made to go into a bedroom where strangers slept of a night. On asking Mr. Paine if he heard any noise in the night, he replied he did not. On the arrival of my husband he was quite surprised to find me sleeping in the next room adjoining the one we occupied. On asking me my reason for changing and receiving no other satisfactory answer than I did not like to sleep in that room, he laughed and said, "I expect you have seen Mr. B, who they say is a constant visitor at this place. If he is anywhere about I should like to see him and shake hands with him," replied my husband, "as myself and him were always good friends in his life time." I said, "I hope if there are such things that God will permit you to see them, that you may not be hardened in unbelief, and let you know there is nothing impossible with God." I know that my husband did not believe in anything supernatural.

Mr. T slept in the room alone and was not very well for a few days after he came home; therefore, he did not rest well. The third night after he came home, about midnight, I heard him say, "Mr. Paine, come in my room. Come quick!" He then called Malinda to bring a light, as she slept in my room. Malinda not waking, I got up and lit the candle, and went into my husband's room. He was sitting on the side of his bed as pale as death. Mr. Paine entered at the front door at the same time I came in with the light at the other door, being afraid to go into the room in the dark. When Mr. Paine came in, he entered pistol in hand and looked very much frightened. I asked Mr. T what was the matter. He replied, "A few minutes ago there was a man in the room. As the moon shone full upon his face and I saw it plain enough to know who it was." He said it was Mr. B. "Are you not mistaken," I said. "No," he replied, "I have heard a noise in that bedroom all night, like someone getting out and in." "I was up in the night," continued my husband, "and something brushed my feet like a cat." I laughed a little at this last remark and said, "Perhaps it was a cat." But a search being made, no cat was found. Mr. T said that as soon as the light appeared, Mr. B disappeared. Mr. T and Mr. Paine had laughed not a little at my having seen "the old man," as they called him. I could now laugh at them in return. As they were both too afraid to sleep alone, they both came in my room to sleep, and it was a week before Mr. Paine could be prevailed upon to sleep in his own bed under the stairs. My husband never jested with me or anyone else after this about ghosts.

I had written to my uncle in England to send me some crockery ware, a carpet and some soap and some other things, which I had now received, and was much surprised on receiving a tierce of earthen ware. As I did not want so much, I suppose my uncle thought I could dispose of it to advantage in Texas. On examining it I found to be of the best quality of Liverpool delf, with six dozen of different size dishes and plates, a full set of bedroom service, a set of handsome tea and coffee were embossed with gold. I was made up, I thought, for years for crockery ware. Little did I dream of coming events. The carpet was brilliant Brussells, too splendid for my furniture and house, so I went with my husband to Brazoria to sell it to Mr. R. Mills, a merchant, for goods that would be more useful. It brought $100. and cost seventy-five so I made a little profit.

Not many months after the war of thirty-six broke out, my husband determined to stay as long at his home as possible and work his crop, his prospects being good. My husband had one of his arms broken in two places by the fall of a tree, which disabled him so much he could not do good and efficient service, but sent his overseer, Mr. George Paine, as his substitute. Mr. Paine was about thirty and was killed in the massacre of Fannin's army. I was sorry when I heard of his death, for he was a worthy young man.

It was spring time, nature smiled, the beautiful prairie flowers put up their heads beneath the leaves of green. The jessamine covered lattice, and the atmosphere convinced me of the future resurrection of the body after death. All was sublime. I was quite happy in my home with my husband and child, but suddenly doomed to be the reverse. My husband came home one morning looking sad; no smile lit up his countenance as formerly. He then informed me, as of necessity, of what he expected would be our fate in the issue of the war in our country, the loss of everything but life and perhaps that also. I heard him through; he had portrayed a dismal picture of coming events and had determined to stay on his place till the enemy were in sight, or within a few miles of his home. I begged him to carry me and his child to a place of safety, but he seemed deaf to my entreaties, something he never had done before. He would generally do whatever I wished. He seemed governed by an evil spirit about this time, for all his neighbors for miles around him had left their homes and plantations two weeks before we were compelled to leave.

One evening about sun down Mrs. B's overseer, who worked about one mile from us, came and informed my husband that the Mexican army were ready to cross the Brazos River next morning and that we could not remain any longer at our home. We must stay a sufficient time to cook a little provisions and get up the horses which had all been turned out for the night. Everyone was now in the utmost confusion. The Negroes were told they could take only one change of clothes with them, myself the same. The enemy were only seven miles from us, and it would not do to take anything that would retard our progress. I packed up our china set and put them in the wagon, and thought my husband would think that they were my little boy's clothes and mine, a foolish thought. I took some letters and papers belonging to my father and mother, all the remembrance I had of them, and some other mementoes, which did not take up much room, put them in a Mexican traveling bag and hung them on the horn of my saddle. The boys were sent after the horses and mules, the women were cooking some provisions, and everyone was busy as a bee.

I had no time for the reflection which was, at this time, perhaps for the best. The Negroes were all in tears at the prospect of losing their all, which was felt by them as much as we felt our loss. My husband had about four or five hundred head of cattle, four or five hundred head of hogs, one hundred bales of cotton, fifty at his gin, fifty in the hands of a merchant, Mr. R. M of Brazoria. I had five hundred head of chickens, a good many of which were killed and cooked for our travel that night. At day break we started. I shut the doors, though my husband told me it would be of little use. "Before night," he said, "everything in the house will be sacked." My husband helped me on my horse, a tear came unbidden in my eye. I dashed it from me; my husband saying to me as he gave me the horse's reins in my hand, "Go on my child, and do not look back," which advice I did not obey, having to look back several times after I left the house with a heavy heart.

We stopped about four o'clock in the evening on Oyster Creek. It was too early to camp, but a great many families had stopped for the night, having heard a report that Indians were killing families going the lower route to the Sabine. The men were getting ready to go off and see if the report was correct, whilst the women and some old men with the Negroes were left in camp until they returned in the morning. Mr. T had to go also. I met with my friend Mrs. W on the camp ground.

About six o'clock in the evening as everyone was busy cooking supper, we heard an Indian yell. Everyone listened with the greatest excitement expressed in their countenance. It was heard again and again. Everyone ran to the canebrake, which was close by. In a few minutes the camp ground was cleared of everyone. Myself and friend got into the hollow of a tree, not one hundred yards from the camp ground. Here we remained all night. At nine o'clock, as near as we could guess the time, having heard no more yells, I insisted on going to the camp ground to get a cup of coffee and something to eat, as I had not broke my fast since early in the morning. My friend remonstrated with me on such a course, as she was afraid some of the redskins might be hiding behind the trees, but I could see everything on the camp ground through some holes in the tree. The camp-fires were dying out and lent a melancholy glare. I saw nothing moving.

I slipped off to the camp ground, watching with the eagerness of a cat that is expected to jump upon his pretty. The coffee pots had nearly boiled dry; the meat was most of it burned, but I got enough for my friend and myself; and when about to return to our hiding place, something touched me behind. On looking around, a large black dog was on my dress. He was wishing me to make friends with him. When I did, I nearly let all my provisions fall. Though no cry escaped my lips, yet I was much frightened. He had been left by his owners and was glad to find someone to acknowledge him. On my return we both ate heartily and the coffee was grateful to both. Although my friend affirmed she could not eat anything before I left for the camp ground, her fears for my safety were the reasons for these remarks. We spent a lonesome night of it. No one knew of our hiding place but ourselves.

About four o'clock in the morning we heard the tramp of horses first; they came nearer and nearer, until looking through the hole in the tree I saw one of our men approaching. My heart beat quick when they went on to the camp ground and saw none of us. They said, "Boys, someone must have been here; they have been gone since last night." On seeing it was our men we came out of our hiding place and told them all that had transpired since they left. Some got down and got a piece of meat and bread; others proceeded right to the canebrake where, in trying to follow them up, only run them further in the woods and cane. It took them until mid-day to get them all together and ready to go on our travel.

After starting we traveled all day and all night that night, our enemy fast approaching us. In a few days after we left home, the oxen traveling too slow to keep up with the rest, my husband overhauled the wagon and threw out something belonging to the Negroes which he had told them not to take, and the little trunk with my china was found and set upon the roadside. I entreated to take it along, a foolish request, but to no purpose. "My child," said he, "do you wish to be taken a prisoner? For we will all be taken if we do not travel faster than we are doing now. You have thousands of dollars behind, independent of that little trunk of china." I knew what he said was true, but I kept a sullen silence for several hours afterwards.

The roads in places were impassable and so bad that five or six teams of oxen were put to one, so as to enable us to travel faster and to assist one another through bad places. We traveled in a body so as to be able to resist if attacked. It was not safe for one or two families to travel together. We were about one hundred families together. The men were home guards, some, like my husband, disabled from other battles from being in active service.

The Sabine River was considered the line between Texas and the U.S., so that in case we were overpowered by the Mexican army, we would be ready to cross over into the U.S. The ferry boats had most of them been taken away. Only on the Trinity River, the Sabine, and Neches do I remember seeing a ferry boat. Most of the women and children were carried upon rafts, but myself and husband crossed upon our horses. I thought many times I would be drowned, my horse sinking with me and almost out of sight. It was a wet spring, the prairies full of water, and in many places up to the saddle skirt of my horse. My clothes and feet were wet every day for weeks. It was only when we stopped for the night I could dry them by the camp-fire. I hobbled my horse at night, unhobbled him, saddled him in the morning, unsaddled him at night. Everyone had his own horse to attend to. My little boy rode upon my lap; sometimes I found myself fast asleep on my horse, and only when I was nearly over the horse's head, I awoke to the sense of danger with my little boy in my lap. Notwithstanding, I slept. I held him with a deathlike grasp, and when aroused, I got off my horse, and taking my little boy in my arms, I walked until I was aroused from my slumber.

During our travel, I never slept at night, as either the Indians or the Mexicans were on the lookout for our horses. At night several watchers were put on guard to watch the horses, yet notwithstanding our vigilance, three or four horses would be missing. Mr. T, like myself, never slept, only at noon when the Negroes got dinner and the horses were turned out to graze, and then only slept for a short time. This was all the time I got to sleep myself. When we were called to dinner my husband rose and ate his dinner, but I never got up until the folks were all moving, took my bread and meat in my hand and ate it on the way. I often provoked my husband not a little in being so hard to wake at dinner time. I had lost so much rest that I found it almost impossible to wake when I was called.

One day, after being called a great many times and paying no attention to their call, my husband took his boy and left me asleep on the camp ground. When I awoke, hearing no noises and looking around, everyone gone but my horse, which was quietly grazing not far from me, hobbled as I had always been accustomed to doing him when we stopped for a meal. I looked around as one in a dream. The encampment was all gone, not a soul remained. Could it be real or was I still asleep? My husband had never treated me unkindly. Could it be possible he had gone and left me alone? Or had he not had a chance to wake me? Had some Indians scared them from the camp ground? My boy was gone also. The truth flashed across my brain. He had done this to punish me not to play the same thing over again.

Quick as thought I rose from my resting place, put on my bonnet, which I had taken off for the purpose of resting more easily, and went to my horse, which was a very gentle animal and knew his rider. I was not a minute in putting on the saddle and taking off the hobbles, and in one more minute I was on his back seated. I did not have to use my whip; he knew my voice, and we flew across the prairie, not knowing the road, but trusted to my horse to take the right track, for there were few roads in

Texas those days. After traveling one hour as fast as my horse would carry me, I came in sight of the wagons. I halted to take my breath and rest my horse who was in a foam of perspiration. I was so much put out with Mr. T's treatment towards me, I kept in the rear of the wagons until they stopped at night, and when compelled to stop at my own camp-fire, I looked what I felt, hurt to the core.

My husband came to help me down off my horse, but I refused his assistance, looking not a little displeased. "My child," said he, looking at me, "I know you are angry with me, but I had to do something to alarm you or you would have given me a great deal of trouble in the future." I told him I had been woman enough to pass through trials that a man strong in physical strength alone could pass through and that he need not doubt my mental faculties any more than my physical ones, that I myself was the last consideration in danger, that I thought only of him and my child, but that now I began to think him lacking in his affection for me. After many times professing his love for me, he kissed me, and we went to supper. My little boy was glad to see his mama once more, and I tried to pass off my day's adventure as good naturedly as possible, and my husband seemed all smiles.

I forgave him. Like the Indian, I did not forget this adventure, always telling my husband he was a different man, that the war had changed his nature. He admitted this to some degree, and I was willing to make every allowance for any departure from his usual way of acting. One day we had to pass a bad creek or river. He and his

horse passed over, finding difficulty in getting out, it being
a miry place, saying nothing to me whose time it was to
cross over next. He had always given me instructions
when we came to a bad place. Seeing the difficulty he had
in getting across, I turned around and saw several gentlemen ready to cross. One of them was Mr. T. W, one of
my husband's friends and neighbors when living on Caney
Creek. "Where is your husband?" he called, "passed over
and left you behind?" "Yes sir," I replied. He called to
a gentleman, a friend of his, and said, "Sir, please see this
lady across safe. It is a lady who has got no husband." I
blushed at this remark and felt that he had left room for
such to be made in his haste to get along in his travel.
Many families were behind but not a half mile distant.
So we all moved on en masse, each man who had families,
father or son, seeking to protect his wife and children from
the invaders.

After traveling two weeks with the main body of
families on the way to the Sabine River, we left the encampment in company of ten men, as my husband wished
to carry his family right into the U.S. and leave Texas
for good.[18] He had no hopes of our ever gaining an inde-

[18] Mrs. Sidney C. Covington, in her thesis "The 'Runaway
Scrape': An Episode of the Texas Revolution" (15, 41–42), writes
that although Houston had sent reassurances to the residents of Brazoria, citizens, upon learning that Houston had begun to retreat, also
began to leave. In their flight, Texans "headed for Louisiana, travel-
ling first to Buffalo Bayou, and on to the San Jacinto River. Crossing
here, they made their way eastward to the Trinity. This further retreat
of Houston's army left all the settlements between the Colorado and

pendence, and many circumstances which happened on our travel made him disgusted with the country; and although I begged and entreated him to go back to our plantation when news came that we had gained our independence, I could not prevail with him to return.

One evening two men slipped up on my husband and said, "Mr. T, you are anxious to leave Texas, and you owe me fifty dollars on that little girl you bought of me. If you do not pay the money, I must have the girl as security. This was my little boy's nurse, a girl about ten years of age. When I saw my husband was going to let him take the girl, and she crying most pitifully at the prospect of being separated from me and her master, I stepped up close to him and said, pistol in hand, "If my husband chooses to let you have that girl that is paid for up to fifty, I will not. You must kill me first." My husband walked up to me and took the pistol out of my hand, saying at the same time he could tend to his own business as long as he lived. Soon after the men left with their charge, crying at the top of her voice, my blood boiled with indignation, and as he was about to depart, he said, "Madam, you ought to be the man such times as these. You could defend yourself and property well if you had no husband. I should not have taken the girl from you,

the Brazos rivers unprotected, and the people living in this section of Texas at once began to make their way toward the Louisiana line, and to Galveston Island."

In their eagerness to escape, many residents left food on the tables and their doors open. Some failed to carry enough provisions to last them during their trip.

for I believe you would stay in the country and defend yourself and property."

After being admonished by my husband for my interference in his business we traveled on, one Negro less. In one week, just before we arrived at the Sabine River, two other Negroes, men, went the same way. Then just before we crossed the river four others ran away to the Mexican army, being promised their freedom on doing so. This was seven we lost, two only remained, who were women. My husband was inconsolable at his loss. Nothing that I could say to soothe or comfort him did any good. His temper was so broken that he would break out in a fit of passion on the smallest occasion. At the town of Liberty on Trinity River, he made a sale of his plantation to a man named Moses L. Patton[19] without my knowledge or signature. I did not know he had sold his place in Texas for several years afterwards when I was told by a friend of Mr. T. He sold it for a little over two thousand dollars, and it cost him eleven thousand. It was defrauding his wife and child out of their rights. On asking his reason for doing so, he replied that he thought the Mexicans would

[19] A document in the possession of Mrs. L. G. Rich certifies that Moses S. Patton, witnessed by Benjamin C. Franklin, William P. Scott, and Edmund H. Winfield, on February 24, 1837, sold to Edwin Waller "a certain tract or parcel of land, situated lying and being in said county containing Eight hundred acres more or less, adjoining the lands of W. H. Bynum on the South and Bailey's on the north, the place settled by B. Bailey lately occupied by John Thomas and the same conveyed to Moses S. Patton by the said John Thomas by a deed of conveyance executed in the town of Liberty within said Republic on the third day of April eighteen hundred and thirty seven. . . ."

run the country. It was better to take this two thousand dollars for it than to get nothing.

On stopping at the bayou for the night, after we camped and the horses turned out to graze, the Negroes fast asleep, my husband called me in a low voice to rise, as he was determined to go further that night. On inquiring his motive for doing so, he replied, "I do not like this place. I think I have seen an Indian camp-fire and heard them talking. We must be off as quick as possible, my dear child," and he told me to catch my horse, which I always did during our travel. My husband and servants having to do the same, everyone depending upon himself and not upon another to get ready his own accouterments. Everything was on the move now in great silence. Not a word was spoken, only in a very low tone. The bayou was to be crossed, which was a bad one, banks steep and slippery. My husband gave a few directions in regard to crossing over, our horses slipping down at every step and bogging down to the saddle skirts. Twice my horse fell with me, but letting him have the reins, he rose each time with an effort that might have spoken in praise of a better blooded animal. He was half Spanish and American, named Paton after his owner that Mr. T bought him from. He was faithful, hardy and gentle and seemed sensible to danger and very cautious. Had he not been, I would never have reached Louisiana alive.

Next morning about seven o'clock we reached a town where we stopped and took breakfast. I must state in going through some fine timber, which was twenty miles through, we found the woods on fire, and in trying to avoid the fire, we lost the road. We were three days in this timber before we got out. On the third day, about mid-day, we met a man with some sheep. We stopped and asked him if he had anything to eat along. He said he had a side of bacon, that he could get bread where he was going. My husband asked him to sell it to us, as we had eaten nothing but some small mutton cane and green persimmons for three days. He readily agreed to let us take it, and we sat down upon the grass and soon had it all ate up.

That morning near the edge of the timber we found the persimmon tree. We made a fire and roasted them. I thought at the time, it being before we met the old man, they were the sweetest thing I ever ate in my life. My child's mouth and my own were drawn so from eating them I could scarcely talk, and my child would say, "Bite, bite, Mama," and put his hand to his mouth, for it hurt him. We were out of provisions when we went into the fine timber, but expected to get through by night and stop at some house all night where we could get provisions for ourselves and horses. But we were doomed to be disappointed. On the second day I was very hungry, the third day not quite so much so, but had to get to a stump of a tree to get upon my horse from weakness. Had we been one or two more days in the timber without anything to eat we would have died from hunger. The Negroes were in the same condition. My husband seemed to stand it better than any of us. At least he complained less.

The man who was driving the sheep told us to go eight miles and we would come to a house and that his son lived there, who would supply us with food for ourselves and horses. We arrived there about early dinner time. He treated us kindly and supplied us with food for ourselves and horses. We remained overnight with him and left the following morning, considerably refreshed. Many and great were the dangers we met with, owing to the high water and heavy rains. Many nights I had to lay out in the heaviest rains, for sleep I did not until we were in the U.S.

On our arrival at Negroville, now called Washington,[20] we got on a steamboat and went as far as Doneson-ville[21] in Louisiana. My husband thought this would be a good place to get ourselves as he had nothing left but a few horses and two Negro women and five hundred dollars in money. This was part of the money he sold his land for. Five hundred more he paid Mr. T. W for an injury sustained by a Negro man belonging to Mr. W by a Negro woman belonging to us, who cut her husband with an axe in the back. He had the man's doctor bills, and

[20] Washington is a community in the Saint Landry Parish of south central Louisiana, settled before 1820 and incorporated in 1836. The town was also known as Niggertown because of the large Negro population. It is located on Courtabeau Bayou near Opelousas. John D. Winters, *The Civil War in Louisiana*, 233, and Leon E. Seltzer (ed.), *Columbia Lippincott Gazetteer of the World*, 2065.

[21] Donaldsonville, La., is in Ascencion Parish, twenty-seven miles south-southeast of Baton Rouge. Founded in 1806, the community was incorporated in 1822. *Ibid.*, 525.

when he found my husband determined to leave the state of Texas, he demanded half the value of the Negro man, which Mr. T paid.

I must state that Mr. W had always been a good friend to Mr. T and family and did all in his power to induce Mr. T to return to his home as soon as the war would be over. Mr. W always thought we should gain our independence, but when he found he prevailed nothing with my husband, as a last strategem and resort, he thought perhaps to stop him by telling him he had to pay the five hundred dollars. Mr. T did not forget this act of his friend for a good while, and before he departed this life, for he departed a Christian and died in peace and charity with all men. One trial after another was our lot, loss after loss whilst we remained in Texas. My husband said he did not wish to remain in such a cut throat country, where there was no law but the pistol and bowie knife.

I felt much at my husband's losses but was not possessed of the faculty of comforting him in his misfortunes, although I did everything in my power to console him, bore with patience not only his displeasure but our privations, since the loss of our property:—50 bales of cotton left at the gin, 50 in the hands of our merchant, for when the enemy came into the country Mr. R. M would not advance a dollar on our cotton,[22] our cattle, household

---

[22] In a letter to Governor Oran M. Roberts, Ann wrote that she had applied for financial assistance through the veterans organization, "during those times Mr. Bryant was secretary." Bryant, she noted,

is a great friend of Mr Robert Mills formerly Banker at Galves-

goods and chattels. And the finishing touch of desolation was accomplished when my husband sold land worth eleven thousand for two thousand—his plantation and home in Texas.

> ton, and I have good reason to think that Mr Bryant, was impressed by Mr R Mills to do nothing in my favor, as Mr Mills bought the land that belonged to my husband, on the Brasos river of Mr M L Patton, a quick claim deed for 2050 it cost 9000, thousand my husband bought it of Mr Edwin Waler a vetren, and now liveing, and as I did not sign the deed of sale, he has always been afraid I would I try to obtain my right in it. Mr Mills was my husbands merchant at the breaking out of the war and when the Mexican army came into the Country, he had, 100 bales of Cotton of my husbands in his hands, all of which he sold and never gave us one cent for it, it bringing 20 Cents a Pound at that time my husband was owing Mr Mills 1900 dollars when the war broke out 50 bales was already in his hands when we left for the Sabine line, and he confessed to me Personaly, that he halled the other 50 off after we left, to secure himself for the 1900$ my husband was indebted to him. Those your excellence are grave reasons for my not prospering in the legislator. Mr Mills has friends, money, whilst I a poor widow have but few.

Ann Raney Coleman to Governor Oran M. Roberts, July 25, 1880, Asbury Papers, University of Texas Archives.

Legal papers in the possession of Mrs. L. G. Rich show that A. G. and R. Mills, "merchants and partners" appeared before Hon. Benjamin C. Franklin, judge of the Second Judicial District of the Republic of Texas, indicating that

> they have now pending before your court a suit against an John Thomas an absentee from this Republic That in the said suit they have had seized and attached the tract of land upon which the said Thomas lately resided, That since the obtaining of that seizure they have been informed of the existence [of] other property of the said Thomas in this county of a personal and move-

able nature to wit of horses hogs cattle &c, that upon the land attached at their insistence there is a mortgage, made for the security of the payment of a debt due Mr. Edwin Waller.

The debt, brought out in this legal document, signed by R. Mills and John Paine was $1,500. Atttached to the petition was a note to R. I. Calder, sheriff of the county of Brazoria: "You are hereby commanded to seize and attach so much of the personal and moveable property of John Thomas as can be found in your county as will be sufficient to secure the payment a debt for nine hundred and fifty eight dollars with interest, &c, as set forth in the petition."

Fourth Book

After landing at Donaldsonville, we stopped at the principal hotel. In a few days Mr. T met with a gentleman of the name of Bishop who engaged him and his two Negro women to work for him. He was to open a canebrake plantation in the woods or timber for him on Bayou Grosted.[1] He was to be found for provisions for himself and family. On our arrival at Mr. Bishop's place, which we set out for without delay, we found a small house to live in and about one acre of ground cleared round the house, the most desolate spot one could imagine. We remained there several months without receiving provisions or even a line from Mr. B. Our living was very hard, bread and meat, sugar and coffee. My husband had always been a good provider, but he was now in different circumstances. He was no longer able to live in the way we had been accustomed to. My health was bad and I could not eat the food set before me.

[1] Bayou Grosse Tete is a community which received its name when French explorers in the area discovered a large skull. The community was settled in the early 1830's. Alcee Fortier, *Louisiana*, I, 570.

One day the table was set for dinner and the eatables on it, Mr. T on one side of the table and myself on the other, when in walked a strange gentleman. "Mr. Thomas, I presume?" "Yes, Sir." "Your wife, also." "Yes, Sir." "My name is Austin W.[2] I live across the bayou and have just arrived on my plantation and hearing from my overseer that you have commenced to open a plantation for Mr. B, I have come to see how you cut cane." My husband told him if he would only wait a few minutes, as soon as he ate dinner, he would go with him. "Well," said Mr. W, "Mr. Thomas, have you nothing better to eat than what is set before you? "No sir," replied my husband. "I have been promised provision but they have not arrived, and I fear they never will arrive. Mr. Bishop is not going to be up with his contract."

After Mr. W looking several times at me, I think he felt sorry that one in as poor health as myself had no better living. He was much pleased with the way my husband cut cane and said, "Mr. Thomas, if you like, I will employ you as my overseer and give you fifteen hundred dollars a year, and you will be able to live on my place like a fighting chicken. Your wife's situation requires more comfort than you can have at this place. I will hire your two Negro women and give you a fair price for their hire,

[2] Austin Woolfolk, who at one time owned the Center and Sunny Side plantations, was one of the largest sugar producers in Louisiana. Sunny Side, on the east bank of Bayou Grosse Tete, was nearly opposite Isaac Erwin's Shady Grove plantation. William Edward Clement, *Plantation Life on the Mississippi*, cutline opp. 97, 173–74.

and I will allow your wife fifty dollars a year for cutting the Negro clothing, and all the clothes she wants for herself she can have out of my store house for giving out the provisions and looking after the little children." My husband accepted at once of his offer, but we did not leave Mr. Bishop's place for one month after Mr. T was engaged by Mr. W. Mr. W went home and sent a servant loaded down with all kind of nice provision and some delicacies.

I must now say something about our woman Eliza. She had a white swelling on her lip which caused her much pain. She was very insolent to myself. So one day, I having been misused by her, I said in a fit of passion, "I hope you may die and I will be rid of you, for you make me very miserable." She only laughed at my remark. One night she was sick and my husband gave her a dose of Calomel and bid her at her peril not to drink any water. About midnight, feeling very thirsty, she got up to get some water, and finding none she went to the vinegar barrel and drank all she wanted. She took the cramp in her stomach. We put her up to the neck in a warm bath, but we could only keep her there a short time, for she was getting weaker and weaker. We laid her on her bed. I asked her if she felt better. She replied she did, but they were the last words she ever spoke. Eliza was dead; remorse took possession of my soul. Had I not wished her dead? I begged God in prayer to forgive me and determined never to wish such a thing again. I had been much tortured in my feelings with regard to this woman. She was ever insolent and overbearing in her treatment and conduct to myself. She was a bright mulatto and quite handsome as a Negro. She was buried and I repented sincerely of the wish I made.

We now got ready and moved to Mr. W's plantation. After becoming acquainted with all I had to do, I went about my work cheerfully. Mr. W was kind and pleasant, and as to good living, we lived as well as the richest man in the state of Louisiana. Mr. W, who only came upon his plantation about twice a year, gave everything in charge to my husband, except the dwelling house, which contained a large store room full of dry goods and another room full of provisions, all of which was given in charge to myself to give out to the Negroes when needed. He was a lavish provider at all times for both his Negroes and his overseers, but nevertheless his hands had to work hard. When sick, they had good care taken of them and kindly treated.

There were but few little children on the place when I first went to Mr. W's. Perhaps they might have numbered fifteen or twenty. In one year after I went there there were fifty. This pleased Mr. W much, as they had never raised as many before in the same time. They had never had the attention they needed until now. They were all as fat as little pigs, clean and well clothed. The Negroes numbered one hundred. My husband had two plantations to oversee; everything went well though. My husband had to work very hard, sleeping but a few hours a night, having the Negro quarters to patrol until after midnight. He had a Negro driver who was very faithful in tending to business, yet all devolved at last upon my husband for supervision.

I now had an addition made to my family of one more son, of which I was much attached. It was both good and lovely. At eleven months old it faded like a flower from my gaze. It was never sick until taken with its death. It was taken sick about ten o'clock at night with convulsions, and at sun down next evening, it was blooming in hallowed soil where angels to its culture tend. About the same time it was taken sick, which was about ten o'clock at night, my husband saw a vision, a spirit in the person of a young man about six foot high, dressed in white clothes, his shirt beautifully ruffled, they being fashionable about this time. He walked to the side of my husband's bed and looked upon him with a smile on his countenance. My husband asked him what he wanted, but he did not speak but went out at the door he came in at, the door making a great noise as it closed behind him. My husband did not tell me of this circumstance until a week after my child was buried. The same week it died I had named it after my oldest brother, not knowing that my brother was dead. In a short time after the death of my child, I received a letter from my uncle in England, saying that my brother had been dead six months. I now thought that the apparition my husband saw was my brother, who did not wish our child named after him. His death was a new affliction to me.

When my infant son died there was no one to breathe a prayer on his little grave, no white person there but myself and husband; the Negroes were there, also. With my Episcopal prayer book in hand I knelt down and said all the burial service over my own child. No tears stained my cheek; and with a firm voice I said Amen, and arose from my sad talk. I sat all that day calm but in the uttermost despair. Next day the tears fell fast upon my cheek. My heart, surcharged, ran over with bitter grief and relieved me much.

In one year from that time, a new trial awaited me. I lost my oldest boy. I had also an addition to my family of a daughter whom I named Victoria after the queen of England, she being a pious good woman. My husband would rather it had been a boy, but as she took after him in having black hair and eyes, he was willing to be satisfied.

Before we left Mr. W, several unpleasant circumstances occurred which we were obliged to conceal. Mr. W himself was very severe on his Negroes and could not control his temper. He was a terror to all the women who would rather have met a tiger than him when going from their work. He was as a roaring lion, feared by all, and the day of his departure was hailed as a day of rejoicing. His private character will not bear investigating so I will pass on. He once or twice demanded the keys of the store room of me, which I sent him, under pretense of wanting something, then sent me word he could not find what he was looking for, and sent for me to come and get it. I sent him word that as soon as he left the house I would go and get what he wanted. After seeing I was not to be trapped, he left the house and in the future let me get all that was wanted myself. He got very angry two or three times with me to see what I would say, finding fault with everything I did, but on finding me more than a match for him, he let me alone for the future, telling my husband that he liked his wife for her spunk, saying that "All the overseer's wives I have ever had before always cry themselves to death when I scolded them, but your wife, Mr. T, tells me my own so faithfully and truthfully, I am glad to make tracks and get away from her." He had told me his private life which is too bad to write. . . . [3] He was worth, according to his own statement, one million dollars, all of which he made in trading for Negroes.

One evening in the dead of winter the Negro driver had a falling out with Mr. T's Negro woman, Malinda, all the Negro we now owned, she being hired to work on Mr. W's plantation. The woman ran to the house seeking protection from her master, but when the driver stated her offense, she was obliged to let the driver whip her. She was willing to be whipped but did not want the driver to do it, but in finding that my husband would not gratify her by doing it himself, she set off as soon as she received her chastisement to the bayou, which was not twenty steps from the house, and jumped in. My husband did not have any thought about her drowning herself, and when she said she was going to do so, my husband told her to go on, and she was soon over her head in the bayou

[3] A section of the journal has been omitted here.

which was frozen over with a thin coating of ice. It was a very cold night. Some of the men watched her and came and told my husband.

A small boat was put in the stream to try and save her, but life was nearly extinct before they got her out of the water. Three or four hours were spent in trying to restore her when she gave evidence of returning to life. Next morning at day break, before any of the neighbors could have heard of the night's adventure, my husband went to the house of a wealthy planter by the name of Dickinson.[4] He had a few months previous to this time wanted to purchase Malinda of my husband for a field hand, offering seven hundred dollars for her. My husband wanted eight hundred, so no more was said on the subject. My husband was now willing to come to Mr. D's terms. On telling his business, taking care not to reveal the night's adventure to Mr. D, Mr. D, being a notary public, writings were drawn up, sale confirmed and the money paid to Mr. Thomas. On his being seated at the table for breakfast his countenance wore a good natured and pleasant look. I guessed the cause. He ate a hearty breakfast and then called his woman Malinda and told her to get ready as there would be a conveyance after her to take her to her new home, that she was no longer his property. She pleaded with Mr. T to still keep her, as she did not wish

[4] Charles Henry Dickinson at one time was the most extensive real estate owner in Iberville Parish, Louisiana. For many years he was parish surveyor and at one time was mayor of Plaquemine. His map of the parish is still a splendid example of map making. He died in 1846, leaving a wife and three children. *Ibid.*, 75.

to leave us, but it was then too late. Mr. T told her he was too poor a man to run the risk of losing her every time she got into a fit of passion. Should you take a notion to take your life, you cost me seven hundred dollars, and I have just got my money back. She grieved much, at last went, but very reluctantly.

My husband by overseeing had his temper much tried, and when he saw me out of humor with arduous duties on the plantation, would say, "Never mind child, I will have a house of our own before long, and drive my carriage on the Mississippi River banks before I die," which prophecy was certainly fulfilled. Mr. T wished to leave Mr. W but did not like to tell him so, as he had no excuse to leave, only to have a home of his own for himself and family. He was making two thousand dollars clear money every year, had the best of living and everything his own way. His exercise was too much for him, in the field at four o'clock in the morning and twelve at night when he lay down to rest. Cold, rain, or heat, he had to be at his post. He addressed a letter to Mr. W and told him to send a man in January to take charge of the plantation, as he wished to make a home for himself and family. Mr. W was inconsolable at this news. He had thought he could never get a man to suit him like Mr. T. After many intreaties to stay, but to no purpose, we were allowed to depart and another man was sent to take charge of the plantation.

My husband went to Virginia to buy some servants, and I was placed with a French lady to board until he returned. Mrs. Cutware was very kind to me and it was whilst boarding with her that my daughter was born. My husband was gone two weeks longer than he expected. Bad news reached his ears at the mouth of Bayou Placko-men[5] that I was very ill and not expected to live. The report, which was false, excited him so much that he got a man to bring his Negroes up the bayou in a boat, and he started off on foot to walk thirty miles. When he arrived at Madame Cutware's he was more than glad to find me well. Two days after his return, my daughter was born.

The four years my husband was overseer for Mr.W he made seven thousand dollars. With this money he bought nine slaves, four women and five men. In a month after the birth of my little girl we moved to Mr. W's upper plantation housekeeping for ourselves. Mr. T had contracted with Mr. W to open another plantation with his own hands, Mr. W giving him half of all that was made on it, furnishing the team and all the farming utensils. It was no small job to undertake to open a plantation through the thickest kind of canebrake, infested with panthers, bears, wild cats and many other wild animals.

My husband was an expert bear killer and I often feasted on this kind of meat, which was very sweet. Mr. T and myself had been out spending the day with some of

[5] Plaquemine is French for persimmon, and the village bearing that name is situated on the west bank of the Mississippi River. The town was made the seat of government for Iberville Parish in 1835 and by 1837 was the banking center of the area. The Bayou, next to the Atchafalaya River, was the largest outlet for waters of the flooding Mississippi. *Ibid.*, 97–98, 180.

our friends in the bayou. On coming home in evening through the canebrake, I spied a bear, a formidable animal. I ran back a few steps with my baby in arms, when my husband told me not to go away. After watching him a few minutes he went into the woods and gave us the road. Mr. T took the baby in his arms and proceeded on, but I was much alarmed. He was after some hogs, so he did not trouble us. One of our Negro women was taken sick. My husband went out to get his horse, but the night being dark he could not find him. He came back with a very long face and asked me to get along the best I could. Before day a little boy was born; he was a fine child who lived and prospered. Not many months afterwards a little girl was born into this troublesome world.

A panther hunt was being in agitation by our neighbors, who were feasting daily on their hogs. I was requested to get wood and water in the house sufficient to last two or three days, as it was considered dangerous to be out of doors about this time, as he might attack the first person he met when hunted down. A large one had been in the habit of coming to our garden of a night and eating the tomatoes which grew there in abundance. On the second day's hunt they killed him. He was ten foot long and was eating part of a pig when they came upon him. He showed fight, but as there was a good many of them they soon dispatched him.

We were not relieved from our confinement. There was another animal very annoying to us in this wilderness which was the alligator, which lived mostly in the bayou, but as soon as I put any clothes on the bushes to dry, they would come out of the water and carry them off. I had three red flannel coats carried off by these reptiles belonging to my baby, and I suppose I never should have known what became of them, had I not seen one come out of the water and take it off the bush as I was going to the bayou after water. After he got his prize, on my approach he darted under water and was out of sight. The mystery was solved what got my clothes. I put no more there in the future.

About this time I was taken sick with a disease I never had before, a breaking out all over my body which went into sores. My husband sent for medical aid who pronounced it the heat. He told me to wash in flax seed tea, which I did, but on the inflammation coming to the surface of my skin, it swelled my limbs to such a size I could not walk or set a foot to the ground. I could not bear any clothes upon me and I lay without between two sheets. I was confined two weeks to my bed. During my illness my oldest boy Edmond took sick, yet I could not prevail upon him to lay down. He complained of his head hurting him and had some fever. He kept round playing most of the time by the door outside the house.

On the third day at night, as he was going to bed and was no better, my husband gave him a dose of calomel, which was followed by a dose of oil. Before day, the Negro woman who waited upon him came to my bed and said, "Edmond is black about the mouth, Ma'am." This information startled me and I sent her to bring him to my bed, prop me up first with pillows. She did so and brought the child to me. Death was on his face. She laid him in my lap, and I said to him, "You are very sick, my dear boy." His reply, "Mama, I cannot stand this long." I sent for his father who was in the field with his hands. He came quick. "Mr. T," I said, "our boy is dying." He was shocked and spoke to him. He turned his eyes upon his father and repeated the same words he said to me, "I cannot stand this long." In one minute after this he closed his eyes and breathed his last breath without a sign or struggle or groan. He was gone to God who gave him. My husband was not to be reconciled, for he had loved his boy with an ardor only known by a father. For months after his death I did not know how he existed at all, as he ate little or nothing. His countenance was changed. He never smiled. My boy was buried by his father but I was not able to see his grave for weeks, his death retarding the progress of my recovery. His death was caused by congestion of the brain.

After my child died, my sister from the north came to stay with me. She brought her oldest boy with her. She came for her health which was very bad. About this time she had been pronounced in the last stage of consumption by her physician. She had a very bad cough. In a few months she was entirely restored. It being late in the fall when she left her father-in-law's residence, General H on the banks of the Ohio River, she had come in the right time to comfort me for I had need of her sympathies.

A few weeks after my child died, I dreamed of see-

112

ing him in his grave clothes. He extended his little hand to me and said, "Mama, feel my hands." I replied, "No, Edmond, you are cold and dead." He replied, "Mama, I am warm," but I did not touch him. He went off but came back quickly and went to grinding coffee, which he used often to do when living. For me, this time, he had on his usual wearing apparel. He came to me a second time and said, "Mama, feel my hands for they are warm." This time I did feel of them and found them as warm as my own. He then laid down full length upon the floor and asked me to throw a pall over him. I replied, "Edmond, you have one thrown over you." When he said, "throw another," I then threw a sheet over him. "Throw another," he said. I threw something else over him. He asked me to throw another. I woke up; it was a strange dream I interpreted in this way—that he had to be buried in three different graves, which interpretation was fulfilled.

We had made one crop upon the Thomas place, for so everyone called it, although it was not my husband's. He only had a share in the proceeds, and it still goes by that name, he having made the place when nothing but a canebrake.

My sister had an addition to her family of a son who was named after his grandfather William Henry Harrison. In a few weeks after his birth she returned to her husband, Mr. Benjamin Harrison.

In a month after she left we moved to the Mississippi River, Parish Pointe Coupee, where my husband had bought a plantation. We took the remains of our dear boy with us. This was in the year 1840. Four acres were in dispute, but in case the man my husband bought of should lose it, it was to be deducted from the purchase. Unfortunately for us it had the dwelling house on it. In a few months after our arrival at our new home, we were informed by Mr. Robinson,⁶ of whom my husband purchased his place, that he had lost the four acres on which the house stood, and that we would have to build another one. This was a cross to my husband as he was not prepared to spend more money at this time, having paid some five thousand dollars on his land which he bought on one, two and three years time, having laid out his money on the purchase of his slaves, and although cotton was at this time worth twenty cents a pound, he had no way but borrow money to build a house. He, to accomplish this, had to mortgage his slaves and plantation to Mr. Charles Morgan.⁷ He worked 100 hands and was considered a wealthy planter.

I was requested to sign this mortgage but promptly refused for the sum of twenty-two hundred dollars. Neither my husband nor Mr. Morgan liked me refusing

⁶ A William Robinson, thirty-one-year-old planter, was listed in the Pointe Coupee census for 1850. His real estate at the time was evaluated at $6,000.

⁷ Charles Morgan was listed in the Pointe Coupee census of 1840 as head of a household in which resided one male between 15 and 20, two between 30 and 40, and one 60 to 70; and one female under 5, one aged 20 to 30, and one 30 to 40. His holdings included 184 slaves, 115 of whom were employed in agriculture.

to sign the mortgage, and for a few days I was under the displeasure of my husband for refusing to sign my rights away, which I bore with patience, telling my husband that I would rather live in a log cabin than he should mortgage his slaves and land for the borrowed money. This was one step my husband took that proved him in the wrong. In after years it made me a homeless and penniless widow.

The place we lived on had been a stopping place for travelers for years, it being immediately on the coast or river. This was one reason Mr. Robinson sold to my husband, finding himself obliged to take people in for a night, his wife having delicate health could not attend to them. He determined to move where he and family would live more private, but took good care to say nothing about this to Mr. T before he bought the place. We soon found that we should be obliged to take travelers in, for they would stop, it mattered not what kind of accommodations they had; but my husband bought some mattresses and we laid them all over the sitting room floor of a night. Money was plentiful then, two dollars for a man and his horse at night. We often had from eight to ten persons stay all night with us. This was employment for me I had not looked for. My husband's crop was planted and his prospect good.

About three or four months after we were settled, my husband had an attack of inflammatory rheumatism, which confined him to his bed three months. A Doctor Russell, under a pretext to get a little money, told me if I would give him a hundred dollars he would cure him in three days. I promised him to give him the sum if he did so. He remained day and night for three days, but did not perfect a cure, saying that my husband had palsy and rheumatism combined so that a cure could not be made. He left; I paid him the money. It was several weeks after this when the warm weather set in that my husband was enabled to leave his bed. He had hired a young man to attend to his plantation during his sickness, which was a great help to myself when travelers stopt for the night.

My little girl was two years old and a great comfort to me, now my only living child. A lady by the name of Whitaker, who lived a few miles from us, died and left four children, the oldest a daughter sixteen years of age, three boys. Her daughter had just come home from Bardstown, Kentucky, from school, a week before her mother's death. A guardian was appointed for the children and Louisa was placed with us to board and under our protection. My husband had commenced his new house about a quarter of a mile from the river. People in the neighborhood thought my husband foolish for building so far from the river, but my husband said it would not be ten years until the road would run close by the house, but they did not believe this. In nine years after we built our house, although Mr. Thomas did not live to see it, the house had to be moved and the road run fifty yards further back than where the house stood.

A graveyard was selected by my husband to bury

himself and his little boy Edmond, whose remains had now been removed three times in three different graves. My dream was now fulfilled. My boy had shown me by the covering of him three times that he would be moved three times, which came to pass. It was a sad task for Mr. T, but he did it patiently, bringing his remains into the hall of the house to put them in a new box, for the coffin was decayed badly. I looked upon those mouldering bones of my own flesh, which made me sadder but a better woman.

We were boarding a good many carpenters from New Orleans, Mr. Conner being the head man or boss carpenter. Louisa had a small black pony, of which she was very fond of riding, and would often be gone for hours. I remonstrated with her on the propriety of riding alone, as Mr. T would always go with her in an evening. By accident I found that Louisa had an amour with one of the young men helping to build our house by the name of Powers. He was much addicted to drinking. Letters had been passing between them some time through the Negroes. They were head and ears in love with each other before I found it out. Louisa had about three thousand dollars coming to her from her mother's estate. The young men found it out and commenced paying attention to her right away. I and my husband talked to her about him being a very unsuitable man for her. Her mind was made up. She was going to have John Powers for a husband.

I went to the guardian and informed him of what

was going on. He came to see Louisa and told her if she married so unworthy a man as Mr. Powers, he should never have a dollar of her money, for this was all he was marrying her for. Louisa was very good looking, inclined to be stout and robust, cheeks like roses full bloom, of German descent, a well behaved, courteous girl, warm hearted, close in her dealings, and a good housekeeper, tidy in appearance, and very bashful when spoken to. Neither mine or her guardian's advice prevailed with her. I asked him if I should give her a wedding. He replied, "Oh yes, to be sure. If she makes her bed hard she will have to lay hard." There was a vast difference in their appearance. Mr. Powers was a rough uncouth man; she, ladylike in her manners and polite. The contrast was too great for her to be happy. I begged her to think seriously of the subject.

We sent to Orleans for fruits and several other articles for the wedding. The day being set, I went about my task to provide for it with a sad heart, for I had prognosticated anything but happiness for Louisa. He was the first suitor, the first to pop the question, and Louisa, who had no experience in life, thought, of course, she must have him for a husband. The night for the wedding came. Only our nearest neighbors were invited. The marriage being performed, the bride and groom left for another neighborhood, his employer having no further work for him. I felt a little lonely after she left.

One night my husband went to bed as well as usual.

About eleven o'clock at night I heard him breathing very hard. He was not in the habit of doing so. I got up as I slept in another bed in the same room with my child. I called him; he did not answer, so I went and found him wide awake but speechless. I tried to raise him, but he was as helpless as an infant and fell back on his bed. I called my cook and we both tried to raise him, but could not make him sit up. He tried to speak but could not. He had had a stroke was evident. I sent immediately after a Doctor. He got there in a few hours. He bled him when my husband was sensible. He was very ill and lost, by the stroke, the use of one side of his body and for several weeks he lost his speech. For ten days he had the brain fever and it took three of our Negro men to hold him in his bed at times, for he was like a mad man.

On the tenth day after this he was sensible and called me to him and said, "Ann, my child, I am going to die. Send for Mr. Morgan as I wish to settle up my business." The mortgage had run out with Mr. Morgan and he wished it renewed, but when Mr. Morgan came he thought my husband could not live many days and would not renew the mortgage, although earnestly begged by my husband to do so. My husband lived several months after this and the mortgage was renewed. I was again asked to sign it, but still refused, which made Mr. Morgan wrathy.

My husband was now doomed to be a cripple the rest of the time he lived, which was not long, but long enough for anyone to suffer as he did. One morning his

Negro man passed the window with his horse to water. He asked me if I thought he would ever ride his horse again. I replied, "Pa, if you can live through this cold weather," for it was now the month of December, "you will ride your horse again in the spring." "I fear," he said, "I shall not." He looked sad and tears filled his eyes. He made me sing hymns to him often. "When I Can Read My Title Clear"[8] was a favorite hymn of his. He had connected himself about three months before he died. He said it did not look well for a man to belong to a different church to his wife. He was a Baptist, but he said, "Our religion is the same, my child," only he believed in immersion. I believe he was truly converted before he died.

I had the whooping cough, my little girl also, she having taken it first. About eight days before Mr. T died he took a cough similar to the whooping cough. It was not unlikely that he could have caught a sympathetic cough. He was so weak he could not cough up the phlegm, took the fever, and in eight days from this time he was at rest. For two days before he breathed his last, he was in constant prayer and when I went to him to ask if he

[8] "When I Can Read My Title Clear" by Isaac Watts and J. C. Leroy contains the following words:

> When I can read my title clear
> To mansions in the skies;
> I'll bid farewell to ev'ry fear,
> And wipe my weeping eyes.

Homer F. Morris, J. R. Baxter, Jr., Virgil O. Stamps, and W. W. Combs (comp.), *Favorite Songs and Hymns*, 231.

needed anything, he said, "No, do not disturb me." As I laid down one night, exhausted from watching, for this had been my task for seven months, much less the eight days he was so much worse, the spirit told me not to lay down. "Your husband will soon be at rest." A gentleman by the name of Stone, one of our watchers for the night, called me and said, "Your husband is fast passing away." I took my Episcopal prayer book and knelt down at his bedside, said prayers suitable for a dying person.

During this time he had my hand in his; he turned his eyes with a smile upon his features upon me for an instant and pressed my hand, as much as to say, "I thank you, my dear child," which he always called me, and pointed to the bed where our little girl, Victoria, lay asleep. I knew he wished to see her and I went to the bed and woke her and told her her father wished to see her. The child seemed sensible that her father was dying. She sat on his bed at the head. He took her hand in his and she kissed him. Tears filled her eyes and ran down her young and tender face. He was now too far on his heavenly mission to notice anything more. After struggling one hour with the phlegm in his throat, he breathed his last. Not until his spirit had fled to mansions in the skies[9] did my child leave her post, still holding his hand. His last struggle had been almost too much for my nerves, which were shattered badly by his seven months sickness and suffering. I took my child by the hand and lifted her

[9] The phrase is from the first verse of the hymn, "When I Can Read My Title Clear."

from the bed and went into the next room, leaving the last task to be done by friends.

The next day he was buried on his own plantation in the Parish of Coupee in the year 1847. I went to the grave on his favorite horse, which he told me he wished to be turned loose and for no one ever again to ride him. He selected his own burying ground a year before he departed this life. It was by the side of his little son, Edmond, under a mulberry tree.

My health, which had been so bad, began to recruit; my hitherto wan face began to wear a brighter appearance. My widow's weeds, I was informed by my friends, made me look interesting, as I always became black. Eight months had rolled away and there was a gentleman boarded with me by the name of Coleman;[10] also a Mr. Smith[11] of North Carolina who had been with us since we lived on the Mississippi River. Mr. Smith, who in the course of time, became the husband of my sister Mary. He had always been a great assistance to me and my husband in keeping books or transacting business for him, which he was always very ready to do. He was with us when my husband died; also Mr. Coleman. Mr. Coleman had a store, and finding no place so convenient as our house to board, we agreed to take him. Mr. C had been with us two years before my husband died. Mr. Smith still longer time.

[10] John Coleman.
[11] J. Locke Smith.

Mr. Smith was the sheriff of our Parish; he had also filled the office of Clerk of the Court. He was also once a dry goods merchant, but unfortunately he got in business with a man who failed and left him without a dollar. My husband never thought of charging him for board; he was always considered as one of the family. He was always very kind to myself and husband and ready to serve us on any opportunity. I loved him as a brother, not knowing that in the future he was destined to be called by that name.

My property was advertised for sale in the parish paper. This was done by Mr. Morgan, the mortgagee. I got into my carriage and went to see if I could induce him by any fair promise to stop the sale. As I prevailed nothing with him, only in evasive answers, I went further down the river to see a lawyer and asked him if he knew why Mr. Morgan wanted to sell my property at such a bad time. It was now the month of June. "Madam," replied the judge, "he wants to get the chance to buy it all himself for little or nothing." The judge stopped the sale until a proper season should arrive to sell it, as it was advertised to be sold in the spring when the crop was all planted and everything going on well for another crop, out of which I offered to pay the half of my debt. About this time Mr. Coleman seeing me perplexed with my business, offered to loan me seventeen hundred dollars on the mortgage. Having settled this thus far, Mr. Coleman took Mr. Morgan's receipt, put it in his pocket, but did not have it recorded on the court house books in our Parish where we lived. I was sorry in the extreme after this was done, for it was not very long after this act of kindness was performed for me until Mr. Coleman asked me to let him throw the weight of business off my shoulders on his by uniting in the bonds of wedlock.

Some fifteen persons were invited to our wedding, it being very private, as it was too soon for me to cast aside my widow's weeds and forget that kind husband who loved me dearly, not wisely, but too well. All our neighbors who were independent planters were invited. A nice supper was got up for the occasion. My servants were all sad and bitterly opposed to my marriage with Mr. Coleman. I had known Mr. C three years before my marriage with him and knew but little of him then. He was a stranger who no one seemed to know only from business transactions. He was popular as a storekeeper in the neighborhood, selling groceries and dry goods. A quiet sort of man, a nice man as the ladies termed him, dressed as fine as a nabob, was good looking, all but his eyes, which were small and light blue. Some people termed them pig eyes. He never looked you straight in the face, but always under his eyelids, middle size, dark complexioned, black hair.

Time passed slowly to me. Every three or four days Mr. C would have a fuss with some member of his family. If it was not the Negroes, it was myself. Though my servants obeyed him, they heartily despised him, both for his treatment of myself and them, which at times was unreasonable and unbearable. I had given all my business into his hands to attend to. He knew nothing about the planting, nor would he let the driver manage who understood it well, for he had been under my husband for many years before his death, and he had instructed him so well that Jesse was in truth a good planter and a faithful servant.

About six months after my marriage, I had come to Texas about some land which was my father's, situated on the Colorado River, having fallen into the hands of a man by the name of Burgess,[12] who got the presiding judge by the name of Scott to appoint him administrator of the land. The estate had been administered upon at my father's death, he being solvent and settled up in 1833. But Burgess thinking, because it belonged to two girls, orphans, that perhaps we did not know we possessed the land, as we left the state, and that he might as well possess it as anyone else. This was his excuse.

Mr. Coleman and my sister rode two large American horses. I rode a black pony, a good pacer as well as a fast traveler. The first day was my most unfortunate one. The Mississippi River was in many places over its banks or levee. We were compelled to deviate from the

[12] Ann probably refers to John Burgess, a single man residing in Brazoria who purchased property in Lamar, Clay, Wichita, and Montague counties. Files in the General Land Office of the State of Texas indicate that he was especially active in the purchase of property on May 2, 1835, and on March 15, 1838.

right road and go into the swamp to avoid deep water. In one place where there were a great many vines, it was with much difficulty that Mr. C and my sister extricated their horses as their feet became intangled in them. At last they got out. I came next with a presentiment of what would be the issue of my getting through. My pony was strong enough but his legs were too short. He went along well enough until he became intangled in the vines and found himself fast by the feet; he made one spring to clear himself and was brought down flat to the ground, throwing me several feet in the air against some cord wood. I fell, hurting the back of my head severely and giving me such a shock that nature was dead to all appearances for a few minutes.

My sister and Mr. C saw me fall, got off their horses, and came to my assistance. Fortunately some water was close by. They bathed my temples and head and in ten minutes I was sensible and able to tell where I was hurt. My head hurt me most, which must have been horribly cut but for my long, black hair, braided in one solid knot on the back of my head. I was much bruised inwardly although I did not feel the worst of my fall until on my travel next day. If I could have been bled at the time, I should not have suffered so much in after years. For several years afterwards, in the same month in the spring, I suffered much pain in the head.

In my travel my pony gave me some trouble. In passing through water he took a notion several times to lay down with me, and it was only by using my riding whip very freely I could make him rise. Sometimes when I got in deep water, Mr. C would get behind him and and whip him until he got through the water, giving him no time to study about his favorite trick. He was a May colt, so this accounts for his bad habit. We traveled at the rate of thirty-five to forty miles a day, reaching Texas in eleven days from the time we started. Nothing of much import happened on our travel. Mr. C behaved better than I looked for. Nevertheless, he had several quarrels with me on the way.

When we got to our stopping place at Mrs. Lynch's[13] on the Bernard River, where we had determined to stay and rest our horses ten days before starting back to Louisiana, myself and Mr. C had to go to Matagorda to attend court, a distance of fifty miles further. We started early in the morning. My sister ought to have gone with us but was too sick to go. At sun down we were twelve miles from Matagorda. My horse was tired down. My husband quarrelled with me because I could not ride faster, which I could not do, for both myself and horse were completely broken down with fatigue. "I will leave you," said Mr. Coleman, "if you do not ride faster and

[13] Ann Raney could refer to Anna Lynch or to Fanny Lynch. Anna, wife of James Lynch, was one of the Old Three Hundred of Texas. Her husband received a *sitio* of land in present Washington County in 1824. He died sometime in 1836 or 1837. Fanny, another of the Old Three Hundred, was the wife of Nathaniel Lynch, who received title to a league of land in present Harris County. Lynch died in 1837, leaving his name to the settlement which became Lynchburg. Webb, *The Handbook of Texas*, II, 97.

whip your horse up." He shortly made his threat good and started off at a gallop. He was soon out of sight and I was left to my own reflections. I took this treatment as I did everyone of his acts toward me, patiently. I was sustained by the divine Legislator.

I had laid the bridle reins on my horse's neck, it being now so dark I could not see my hand before me, and as I was unacquainted with the road, trusted entirely to my horse, who I knew could see at night when I could not. I was a little uneasy about a stream I had to cross called Big Boggy.[14] There was a bridge over it without any railing on it and the planks were full of holes so that I felt afraid to cross it. In one hour from the time Mr. Coleman left me, my horse's feet struck something like timber. It sounded hollow. This I took to be the bridge. I reined up my horse and got down. I looked carefully for the bridge and saw the water shining on each side. I took my horse by the bridle, got into the middle of the bridge as near as I could for it was a very dark night, and feeling carefully for my footing, led the horse across. The bridge was a bad one and was in a very decayed state, there being holes large enough for a horse to get his foot on. I felt much frightened whilst going across, expecting to lose my footing every moment. I sent up a prayer to God and He heard me. I and my horse were both safe on the other side of the bridge.

[14] Big Boggy Creek rises in central Matagorda County and flows southeast approximately twelve miles, emptying into Matagorda Bay. *Ibid.*, I, 157.

Here was a difficulty I had not expected. There was no place for me to get upon my horse, no stump of tree, or any means for me to get up. I tied my shawl in the stirrup, letting it down enough for my foot to reach it, and with one effort of determination jumped into the saddle. My horse, though tired, was impatient at the delay, his companion, the other horse, being gone ahead of him and I had little control of him. He seemed to have caught new strength, whilst at every step he made I grew weaker. Nature was exhausted. I longed for one refreshing draught of cool water to cool my parched lips, for I had not tasted water but once that day. My horse traveled an even walk and I let him have the bridle; all was darkness. I was not sure where I was going, but left my destination to my horse. After a few hours ride I saw a star in the distance, which looked like some beacon light to lead me. "It must be the town of Matagorda,"[15] I thought. It grew larger and larger as I advanced. Yet, it was the town and its different lights. I was cheered by the prospect of getting to my journey's end, and but spirit broken, three lonely hours ride on a dark night on a strange road had caused thoughts of the past and future to run with a meteoric swiftness through my brain.

As soon as I got in town I stopped at the hotel. Mr. Coleman came to help me off my horse, and as soon as

[15] Matagorda was established in the 1830's after Stephen F. Austin secured permission to build a town at the mouth of the Colorado River. By 1832 the community had a population of fourteen hundred; five years later it was county seat of Matagorda. *Ibid.*, II, 157.

I got into the parlor, I lay down on a sofa and for a few minutes felt unconscious of anyone's presence. The lady of the hotel stood before me, my husband also. "She must have fainted," said the lady, "for she does not move." "No," I said, "but I am next thing to it. I am so exhausted, my nature is powerless." My husband seemed ashamed, and when he left the room and I had told my hostess how he had treated me, she was more than kind to me. Next day I was confined to my bed all day and the trial was deferred to the day following. I treated my husband with silent contempt. Mutes are generally inoffensive, saying neither good or evil.

After proving our identity, our land was restored to us, and in a few days we set out for our homes. I must now admit a circumstance which took place on my arrival at Mrs. Lynch's on the Bernard. On going into her house and looking around, the first thing I saw was my own dear mother's picture taken in England by one of the finest artists of the day. "Where did you get that?" I exclaimed. "Oh," she replied, "your sister Mary left it with me when the Revolution of '36 broke out and although I lost everything I possessed on returning home to my plantation after we gained our independence, I found the frame in the fodder house, but no picture. Two years afterwards, as I was looking for a nail in an old tool chest that stood out of doors with nothing in it, I saw something shine at the bottom of the chest, and when I picked it up, to my extreme surprise, I found it to be your mother's picture." I felt so delighted that I gave Mrs. L a new shawl and took possession of the picture, being determined to try and take it home with me.

Many of my old friends who heard of my being in Texas sent me word that I must come and see them before I left, but this I could not do as our time was limited. My best friend, Mrs. D. R, was going to send her carriage after me, but I sent her word it would be impossible to see her, as we had determined to start on our journey the very day she proposed to send after me. We left, taking a last adieu of our friend, Mrs. Lynch, who was not satisfied with my second marriage any more than myself and I believe she thought of the frailty of women many times whilst I remained on my visit to her there.

We were two weeks on our journey to Louisiana. The Trinity River being up, we found much difficulty in passing through the swamps. Also in going [along] Little Harah, the alligator holes were very bad. My sister got her horse in one which went over his back, and she might have been killed had he not been a strong animal and able to extricate himself. I turned my horse round for a few seconds as I did not wish to see her killed and hollered to her at the top of my voice to hold on to her horse. He was standing on his hind feet in a perpendicular position struggling hard to get out. Neither myself or Mr. C could render her any assistance. Before we got home we lost a fine American horse. He was taken sick after a hard day's travel and died. We purchased another one before we could go any further.

Fifth Book

My temporal concerns became more and more embarrassed daily, my husband's treatment unjust and cruel. Having occasion to go see my lawyer about Mr. Thomas' estate, which was not yet settled, took the man Jesse to drive me. On my return, he told Jesse if he ever drove me out in my carriage again or came in the yard, he would kill him. The boy told him that he had made his master a promise on his deathbed to do whatever I should ask him as long as he belonged to me, and he was duty bound to fill his promise. Two or three days after this, I was obliged to bind him over to keep the peace, in a bond of three thousand dollars, for menacing me with his guns and threatening to take my life, my last resort for safety, my neighbors and friends advising me to do it.

A week after he bound over, Jesse came in the yard after some milk, which he and all the Negroes were in the habit of getting daily. Mr. C on seeing him shot at him but missed him, one shot going through his hat. The boy ran off the place, being afraid to stay, and I hired him for twenty-five dollars a month to a Mr. Sneed,[1] one of our neighbors. Mr. C had broken his bond and was now liable to be taken by the sheriff. I said nothing about it myself, and so he was still out of the reach of the law. For two weeks after he committed this act, he slept with his arms under his head at night. I asked him why he did so. He replied, "You intend to give me up to the sheriff for shooting Jesse." I told him if the law did not recognize his lawless acts, he might escape his injustice to me.

He said one night late, "Are you asleep?" I replied I was not. "I wish to tell you my dream and see if you can tell me what it means, if you will hear it." I told him to relate it. "I saw your former husband plowing a beautiful gray mare, which fretted and would not go. As soon as your husband got to the turn row, he took her out of the plow and put his saddle upon her and rode her to water, and she went off beautifully. As soon as he gave her water he turned her loose and several persons tried to catch her but could not, and I then went up to her and caught her myself. As soon as I did this I awoke. I wish I knew what it means." "Do you wish me to interpret the dream?" I said. "Yes, if you can." I said, "Well, the gray mare you saw is your wife, myself, which you have treated as a servant and not as a companion. She had been used to the saddle and not to the plow, and when my husband turned her loose and you lost sight of him

[1] The papers of Joseph Erwin mention R. W. Sneed. Alice Pemble White, "The Plantation Experience of Joseph and Lavinia Erwin, 1807–1836," *The Louisiana Historical Quarterly*, Vol. 27, No. 2, 407.

entirely was the time my husband died, and no one else could catch her was the time you married me." He appeared satisfied with the interpretation and said no more that night.

In a few more days he left for the north on business, but previous to his departure he took good care to carry all my riding horses and carriage horses off to a back concession on our land so that no one but himself would be able to find them. He then took out the linchpin of my carriage wheels, so that I should have no pleasure in his absence of visiting my neighbors. He was gone two weeks and during that time I had peace in my family. I went and visited my friends and neighbors and always got sent home in a conveyance, although I had to walk there. He returned a few days sooner than I looked for him. He knocked at the front door one morning a little before daylight. I was asleep but heard the knock. "Who is there," I said. "A friend," he said. "Friends do not often come so late at night," I replied, not knowing the time. "It was not night but day," he said. "Will you let me in?" On this appeal I recognized his voice. I rose and let him in. He seemed in better humor than when he left, but this did not last long.

In a few days after his return, he threw all my nice linen which I had in a large chest into the hearth against the back of the chimney which was full of soot. Being obliged to have a little fire night and morning, I took them out three times, and each time they were thrown back again by Mc. C. At last I took them up and put them

134

in a tub of water. This plan defeated him from throwing them any more. If I left the house to go into the garden for a few minutes and turned the keys in any one of my rooms, he would take his foot and kick them open. In six or eight months after marriage with him there was not a lock upon the place that would fasten or could be used. I had many nice ornaments given me for the house, all of which he destroyed. His chief aim was to break me up and leave me homeless and destitute. With his efforts and the mortgage, this was soon effected. He sold the cord wood on the bank of the river, took the proceeds of our crop and put it in his own pocket, trying to get back the seventeen hundred dollars he paid on the mortgage. He never felt satisfied after he paid the debt. My carriage, which was my own private property, he took without my sanction to get repaired and allowed it to be sold for the cost of the repairs, I myself not having money to redeem it. The cost was eighty dollars. The carriage cost me three hundred dollars.

Debts of the estate as they became due, he allowed the property to be sold to pay its own debts, after putting them off at law as long as he could. After incurring all the expenses to the estate he could, the land and homestead were the first things sold, then the Negroes, and after my property was sold, he would not find me a house and I and my daughter boarded a few months in Bayou Sarah,[2] a little town on the Mississippi River, about

[2] Bayou Sara was one of the principal towns of West Feliciana Parish at this time. Located on the southern part of the parish on the

fifteen miles below our plantation; but the Mississippi River overflowing its banks[3] and coming up into the town compelled us to live for a while in the second story of the house, and my daughter being in the habit of fishing off a plank put there for that purpose, one end resting on the stairs, the other on the fence.

Some boys coming along one day pulling a boat along by catching hold the fence, hit the end which was resting on the fence, causing the plank to fall, and my daughter also was thrown into the water, which was about four feet deep. She held her breath until she rose by the gallery, and making one desperate effort, caught the railing. I was above stairs when I heard the splash of water, guessed the cause, ran down stairs as quick as my feet would carry me, and just caught a glimpse of her head coming up out of the water. I got upon the gallery railing and was

---

Mississippi River, the town was incorporated in 1842 and was an important shipping center. Fortier, *Louisiana*, I, 79. The community was settled when the bayou was forded at great risk by cattle and caravans of covered wagons (*Collier's Encyclopedia*, 521) and in 1850 had a population of 522. Edwin Adams Davis, *Plantation Life in the Florida Parishes of Louisiana, 1836–1846, As Reflected in the Diary of Bennet H. Barrow*, 7.

[3] From Pointe Coupee, Louisiana, J. Locke Smith wrote his brother, W. B. Smith of Spring Grove, North Carolina:

Times are most awfully distressing here. The cholera is making its havoc throughout the country—in this immediate neighborhood many deaths have occurred. One gentleman has lost 4 negroes. Died himself and his child both in the same hour and his wife has been dangerously ill—and expected to die. The nearest neighbor to whom I live has lost two negroes, one last night and

ready to help her by the time she caught hold of the railing. This accident made me so afraid that I determined to leave Bayou Sarah whilst the river was up, the day after the accident. Mr. C came to Bayou Sarah to see me, he having got into a little better humor. He told me he was going to New Orleans and that he wished me to go with him as he thought he could do a better business there than anywhere else.

As my property was all disposed of and I had nothing left, and owing to the neglect of Mr. Coleman not having the seventeen dollars recorded on courthouse books of

one yesterday. And another taken who is not expected to survive —there is no telling what extent we may anticipate its destructive ravages. It seems to be fatal in every case since it has made its appearance in this county, particularly on the coast. Independent of this destroying epidemic, our country is inundated by the overflow of the Mississippi River. The highest waters we have had since 1815. The levees have given way and almost the whole coast from here to New Orleans is now under water—the plantations are crops entirely destroyed. The damage cannot be estimated as it would approximate many millions of dollars—truly the times are destroying lives. I was in the city last night—it presents the dulest aspect that I have ever known. Many failures must inevitably insue—there is scarcely any business doing comparatively with former years at this season of the year. Many steamboats have been compelled to lay up for want of freight. In fact I cannot see how the community or the county can make out. The planters are nearly all more or less involved and have yet their plantion [sic] supply to lay in—the prospect of their crops entirely ruined and cannot expect any accomodations [sic] from the merchants in the city as in former times. . . .

J. Locke Smith to W. B. Smith, May 3, 1849, Manuscript Collection, Duke University Library.

the Parish, which he paid on the mortgage according to law, Mr. Morgan brought in the debt twice over and made the estate insolvent. Yet the Judge said he was clearly of the opinion that the debt had been paid from the receipt which Mr. Coleman had, yet the verdict was against us. My lawyer was Mr. Coleman's solicitor, as well as Mr. Morgan's. How then, my reader, could I expect justice done me? On leaving my home, where I had planted every tree, flower and shrub to beautiful the place, and where my husband and child were buried, my heart was surcharged with grief and a dreary waste seemed before me; but I was cheered on my dark path by the bright smile of a Redeemer's love, one who has said, "though all forsake you, yet will not I."

As my daughter's education was not finished, I determined to go with Mr. C to Orleans, thinking to complete her education at the high school in Orleans as I had not the means to send her to any other. But before we left, my husband got the contract to build a house, which took him about two months to complete, and although we boarded all the hands and I had all the work to do, having lost all my servants, no kind word was ever spoken to me, and once or twice he lifted his hand to strike me, but I got out of his way. We at last started for New Orleans, but not without his making many threats to leave me behind. My sister, Mrs. Mary Smith, and her husband had been living about a year in Orleans and had been boarding in a family. As soon as we arrived, her husband and Mr. Coleman rented a house in partnership, paying the rent in their turn monthly. It was only a few weeks after I arrived there until I was taken very sick. One doctor pronounced me a case of yellow fever; the other, the yellow jaundice.

Coleman had frequently threatened to leave Ann and her daughter while he went to Texas. Finally, while Ann was recuperating from her illness, he carried out his intentions. Ann stayed with a friend, Mrs. F, for several months until she was well enough to support herself and her daughter.

By the recommendation of friends, I at last got a housekeeper's situation in the Veranda Hotel,[4] opposite the St. Charles Hotel.[5] I placed my daughter with her

[4] Verandah Hotel was a family establishment located on the corner of St. Charles and Common and advertised as having the finest dining room in America. Albert E. Fossler, *New Orleans, The Glamour Period*, 14. The hotel was built by James Caldwell, an English theatreman. Robert Tallant, *The Romantic New Orleanians*, 199. An advertisement in the *Daily Picayune* of New Orleans, December 29, 1853, indicated that the "Veranda Hotel" had "undergone complete repairs, &c, during the past summer" and had reopened to the public. Its proprietor, J. W. Young, solicited public acceptance.

[5] The Englishman William Bollaert, visiting New Orleans in 1843, commented that "the St. Charles Hotel is the 'Monstre Hotel' of the South. Its exterior arrangements are upon a very extensive scale and managed with considerable skill and ability. The exterior of this edifice evinces the desire [on the part of] the New Orleans folk to have something classic, but with great deference to them it is not of an architecture appropriate to the character of the establishment or of the climate. The Verandah and the St. Louis Hotels are more in character." Hollon and Butler, *William Bollaert's Texas*, 91.

teacher to board, who was one of the high school teachers. About six months had passed by. Mrs. F sent me word that Mr. Coleman was in the city and had been to her house to inquire after me and requested her to send for me as he wished to see me. I wrote to my friend that I did not wish to see Mr. C, so he went back to Texas. I was now making my own living and educating my child independent of him and passing my time in peace and quiet, although I had a great deal to attend to and my strength was often taxed to the utmost. It was after twelve o'clock at night when I went to rest at night and up at four in the morning. In the month of August the house was closed until the last of September. During this time I was at liberty for a short time to go where I wished. I wanted to sell my half league of land, having found a purchaser provided my husband would sign the bill of sale.

I was anxious to go to England see about some property of my father. Mr. C had written me several letters, all of which I never replied to; but as Mr. Buckley would not purchase my land without his signature,[6]

[6] To the comptroller of the State of Texas from Pointe Coupee, Louisiana, August 1, 1852, Ann Raney Coleman wrote to know

what Tax was dew on the John Raney League Matagorda County you informed it was sold for taxes of 1848, but refered me to the tax collector Matagorda to know if it had been redeemed. I did so, and he informed that it was redeemed by Mr Charls Burkly, who bought the undivided half of my Sister, but refered me to you to know if the Taxes, was not paid on my Part, for the year 1850, 1851, 1852. Mr. Burkly having an agent in Matagorda who paies the Tax on his half you will please let me know if the Taxes have not been paid on my half

I at last wrote him to know if he would sign it. He replied if I would come to Texas and give him five hundred dollars of the money he would sign the bill of sale. My father had settled some property on my mother and her children and on my father being made a bankrupt, it was given up by the trustees to be sold with the rest of the property. But his bankruptcy was one of great illegality and fraud, and as I thought I could recover it, I wanted to sell my land to get money to go on to Europe and attend to it.

I had been two years in Orleans. On the tenth day of June, 1853, I lost that dear and best of sisters,[7] the only true friend I had on earth. This was a fresh trial for me, but as I had known nothing else from girlhood I bore it with fortitude. She died with consumption and was followed to her last resting place by her husband and myself and her only living son, Benjamin Harrison, and my daughter as chief mourners. A few friends went with us to see her deposited in a vault or tomb in the wall of the American burying ground in New Orleans. Her husband was deeply afflicted at his loss. She left her little

as I employed Mr Burkly to pay them if not paid you will please to send me the amount, and I will send you the money as soon as possible. You will please to loose no time in writing me about it and you will much oblige Yours respectfully. . . .

Ann Raney Coleman to the comptroller of Texas, August 1, 1852, Claims Correspondence, Texas State Archives.

[7] The *Daily Picayune* of New Orleans, June 11, 1853, in an obituary column noted the death "on Friday evening at 6¼ o'clock, of consumption, Mrs. Mary Rainey consort of J. Locke Smith."

girl, Alice,[8] who was three years old at the time of her death. The yellow fever was raging with great destruction of life. Every other door had on it a piece of crepe.

I left New Orleans about the middle of August for Texas, intending to return as soon as the yellow fever was subdued, to my business at the Veranda Hotel. All business in Orleans had been suspended and nothing but wagons full of dead bodies were to be seen in the street. My friends wished me to remain, but I told them I was anxious to sell my land. They said I would be more likely to take the fever than if I remained, as I was already acclimated. Their words came to pass.

On my arrival I inquired of the lady at the hotel if there was not a man by the name of Coleman living there. She replied, "Not here, but at Powder Horn[9] three

[8] It was this niece, Alice Smith, for whom Ann Raney prepared her reminiscences and it was she who saved Ann's letters, now in the Manuscript Collection of the Duke University Library.

[9] "The town of Indianola was situated on a narrow strip of land formed by Powderhorn Lake and Matagorda Bay. Powderhorn Bayou is a small body of water that empties into Powderhorn Lake. The lake is about eight miles wide and empties into Matagorda Bay. Major Fryer, a civil engineer who resided in Indianola, believed that Powderhorn Lake and Powderhorn Bayou were once an arm of the bay. He stated that the narrow strip of land that rose in these waters, and on which the town of Indianola stood, was a formation connected with the land at one time."

The town was moved to Powderhorn on the southern end of the island after Charles Morgan, owner of the shipping lines serving the area, built his wharves there, and people began to move into the area which was advertised as Indianola. Powderhorn, thus, was the older name for Indianola. Jessie Beryl Boozer, "The History of Indianola, Texas," 2–3, 19.

miles from here." "How shall I get word to him that I wish to see him?" She said her husband would be going there in a few minutes and he will tell him you wish to see him. Many rumors had been in circulation that my husband had married again, and many believed the report, but I did not, so I said to my hostess, "Is Mr. Coleman married?" She replied, "I think so, and he has sent for his family." This convinced me he had not married to anyone else, but I had had work to persuade my daughter to the contrary. As soon as we were alone she burst into tears and said, "Mama, I am sure Mr. Coleman is married again." "Well, my child," I replied, "so much for the better for me, for I shall not be troubled with him any more."

My daughter was very excited at this time. Neither of us had slept for several nights. Our passage across the Gulf of Mexico was a very rough one, and we were very sea sick. My child had not eaten anything since she left New Orleans. We were both in deep mourning for my sister, whose death had cast a shade across my brow and lent a charm to the features of my daughter, whose black eyes and beautiful suit of black hair with her ruddy complexion, much paler from sea sickness, looked interesting.

The lady of the house asked me if I was a relation of Mr. C. I told her I was. After getting our breakfast, having landed at six in the morning, we both retired to our bedroom for the purpose of sleeping, telling the lady of the house to let us know when Mr. C arrived. We had been resting about two hours when the lady of the house came in my room and asked me if I was the wife of Mr. C. I replied, "If he has not married again, I am." She smiled and left the room, and Mr. C came up to our room. He seemed glad to see us. He kissed myself and child, but I was cold as a marble statue towards him, yet nevertheless polite. I thought of the kiss Judas gave his Master, my dear Saviour. After telling him my reason for coming to Texas and that as soon as he could sign the bill of sale, I was going to return to New Orleans. He would not listen to that; said he had built him a house at Powder Horn and wished me to go to housekeeping. I did not agree to his proposal just then.

He took me and my child to a boarding house for a few days until he got some articles of household furniture in the house. Finding me still determined to return to New Orleans, he would get down upon his knees and beg and cry for me to remain. My heart had been callous by years of harsh treatment. His tears I knew to be like the crocodile's—deceiving. He professed to love me yet he showed me no mercy. He promised never again to misuse me. After many a hard struggle with my heart, I yielded to his entreaties. All went well enough for a few weeks, but he soon returned to his usual way of treating me, often leaving me to provide entirely both for him and my family. I urged him to sign the bill of sale of my land, which he did at last, receiving five hundred dollars of the money.

It had always been the wish of my brother-in-law,

Mr. Smith,[10] for me to take his little girl to raise, but at the time of my sister's death I had no home, no place to take her to, so she remained with her father who worshiped her. News arrived that he was dead, having died three months after my sister. They wrote for me to come and get the child, but as I did not get the letter in time, they sent after her father's brother, who came after her to New Orleans and carried her to North Carolina to his brother's wife, Mrs. W. Smith,[11] to take care of her. She

[10] Mary Raney maried Dr. Benjamin Harrison in Brazoria in 1834. He was thirty-three and she seventeen. Soon after the wedding, Dr. Harrison sent his wife to Ohio, where she remained until after his death in 1840. Nixon, *Journal of the History of Medicine and Allied Sciences*, I, 1, 110–11. The widow then married John Locke Smith and they became parents of a daughter. Mary Raney Harrison Smith died June 10, 1853, of consumption and was buried in New Orleans.

In the Manuscript Collection of the Duke University Library is a letter from New Orleans dated January 29, 1853, and addressed to "Dear Clinton," in which Smith mentions being in the "brokerage and commission business." That he was doing well is proved by his statement that he had made one sale of a plantation and Negroes, the commission of which paid him $850. "I am now about closing another sale of a sugar plantation and Negroes," he wrote, "of which the commission will probably amount to $900."

On a more sorrowful note, Smith wrote:

I am sorry to say to you that my domestic afflictions have been vy great. My wife has been an afflicted invalid for the last twelve months with Pulmonary Consumption. She has not been half a dozen times out of the room for the last year. . . . I see no hopes of her health improving by the treatment which has been pursued. I am now about to place her under the treatment of a celebrated physician of London. . . .

[11] W. B. Smith of Spring Grove, N.C.

was about three years old at this time. I deeply lamented my incapacity to take care of this child, as Mr. C did not always provide for me and would not have agreed for me to do so.

Time hung heavy on my hands. I taught a private school, I took in sewing, yet it was not sufficient to support my family. My life was a burden and but for the grace of God could not have been borne, but my trust in Him saved me from that deep despondency, which without, must surely have been mine. My health was on the decline, and without some change I could not get well, so I informed Mr. C that I was going to England to see after my father's property; that I wished to get the deed for it.[12]

Ann set out for England to investigate her father's estate in June of 1854. In New Orleans, she boarded the Norma, *which was involved in an accident with the* St. Nicholas *near Memphis. Once in New York, however, Ann booked passage on the* Baltic, *a steamship unrivaled on the Atlantic for speed and luxury. The voyage was*

---

[12] In New Orleans, Ann Raney Coleman boarded the *Norma*, which was involved in an accident with the *St. Nicholas* near Memphis. In New York, she booked passage on the steamship *Baltic*, a ship unrivaled on the Atlantic for speed, size, luxury, and popularity. The *Baltic* and her sister ships were the first to offer a complete barbershop, a bell system by which passengers could summon stewards, and steam-heat. Mrs. Coleman's cabinmate for the voyage was the widow of Major Martin Scott, who was killed in the Battle of Molinos del Rey, Mexico.

without incident except that the Baltic *veered once from its course to avoid an iceberg.*

Although delighted by visits with relatives and friends and charmed with sightseeing, Ann failed in her attempt to regain her father's land. In August she returned home.

We left on a steamer for Orleans on our way to Texas.

On our arrival in Orleans, the weather being wet, we could not get round to see my kind friend, Mrs. F, which regretted much. Next day we went on board the *Mexico*, one of Mr. Morgan's steamers,[13] for to go to Texas. We had a rough passage across the Gulf. My daughter never got out of her bed during the voyage, she was so sea sick. I was able to be up most of the time.

On our arrival at Powder Horn, many persons were on wharf looking at the boat landing, Mr. Coleman amongst them. I waved my handkerchief and he caught sight of it, on the instant threw up his hat in the air and cried, "By St. George, there is my wife." In another minute, as soon as the boat was tied, he jumped on board,

[13] In 1855 four regular ships hauled mail from Indianola to New Orleans, scheduled to leave at 2:00 P.M. on Wednesdays and Saturdays, although the owner of the ships, Charles Morgan, had as his motto, "Departures every day be the weather what it may." These ships were the *Perseverance*, under command of Captain H. Place, the *Charles Morgan*, under James Lawless, the *Louisiana*, under W. H. Talbot, and the *Mexico*, under John Lawless. Boozer, "The History of Indianola, Texas," 37–38.

caught me in his arms, then his daughter. After tending to my baggage, we went on shore, everyone supposed me on the missing ship, lost at sea. More than fifty persons shook my hand and congratulated me on my safe return; many persons I did not know or ever spoke to before. We went to Mr. R's where my husband was boarding, for he had unfortunately, on leaving Texas, contracted a debt of thirty dollars and our dwelling house was sold to pay the debt, we both having left the state. I paid the debt out of my own pocket, and after boarding a week we went to housekeeping again.

When Mr. C found I had not received anything from my property in England, his conduct became more harsh to me daily, and the providing for the family depended entirely on myself. My means for living became less every day, and I was compelled to take in sewing for support. On every outbreak of passion of Mr. C I kept silent, for to say anything would only add fuel to fire. If I asked him for means to support the family, he would fly into the greatest outburst of passion, so I quit asking him for anything. Nevertheless, he looked for his regular meals.

One evening my daughter was ready to take a walk out, it being a pleasant evening. We sat down to eat supper. He said to her, "You have been talking against me and I am going to whip you." She looked surprised and denied the charge. When he took hold of her and was about to put his threat into execution, I got up from the table and laid hold of his coat collar and took him into the sitting room and was about to leave the room when he picked up a conch shell that was in the sitting room and threw it at my head before I could make my escape, bruising and lacerating my arm dreadfully. I saw his intention to hurt me and threw up my arm to save my head. I then went into my bedroom and locked myself in. He followed also and was endeavoring to break open the door when some kind neighbors came in and saved me from further abuse. Mr. T accosted him with these words, "I had taken you for a gentleman, Mr. C, before the present time, but I find you unworthy of the name." On showing my bruised arm to Mr. T, he said, "The man who will lift his hand to his wife is not a man, but a coward."

From this I determined to get a divorce from Mr. C. At the end of the same week, I went and saw a lawyer and commenced suit for divorce, which I got first term of court, September, 1855. The dwelling house, the only property Mr. C then owned, was sold according to law, and the proceeds equally divided between us.

I must now state that about one month before our separation, my daughter married Doctor Joseph Waldrop. Their marriage was celebrated at Powder Horn, Texas, in the month of August, 1855, her husband a stranger to both of us. He was handsome man with fascinating manners. It was not surprising that my daughter was pleased and loved him. Young and artless as she was, he was now our only protector. We moved to the town of M[14] on the sea coast. I rented a house and hired a young girl to assist me with my work. The doctor and Sis lived with me for eight months, when they went to boarding, and I, who was not able to keep house any longer, went to teaching a school on G Creek[15] for the sum of six hundred dollars a year, for two gentlemen each having three children. This was in slave time. My daughter had one little girl, which died, and the doctor named it Anna Frances. Herself and husband went north as he thought he could do better business there. I had been teaching nearly ten months and my health was on the decline, yet I did not give up teaching my school.

One day at noon a carriage drove up to the door or gate, and a lady got out. It was my daughter. I could not move. Nature was already weak and I sank back in my chair, for I saw she was alone. I guessed the truth. She had lost her husband. "How?" my reader will say. "Did he die?" No. She met me with tears and a long embrace, at the same time imprinting a kiss on my cheek. After telling me all that had befallen her since we parted, her sorrow and my ill health and physical strength weakened me so that for a day or two I was confined to my bed. But I rallied again, and finding I should be compelled to give up my school and attend to my daughter

[14] Matagorda, the name of which comes from the Spanish *mata* meaning "bush" and *gorda* meaning "thick" or "stout."

[15] Ann probably had reference to the Colorado River, which empties into the Gulf of Mexico in the vicinity of Matagorda.

who needed some comfortable home, for her present situation required it; her husband had left her in a very dependent situation without any means of support.

I therefore settled up my business and went to the town M, where I engaged board for us both. In two month's time she gave birth to a son, who still lives. I then went to housekeeping, having rented a house for twenty dollars a month. I took the public school to teach and sold half a league of land, her father's, to support us at the town of M. My daughter must have seen by this time that my advice to her before marriage was good, telling her it was not safe to marry a stranger, though he treated her kindly as long as he remained with her. In the course of time, she was legally divorced from him. When her boy was four years old, finding I could not get a support at the town of M any longer, I left and went to the town of Lavaca[16] in 1860, and took a house about a quarter of a mile out of town, having got it on reasonable terms and no other being vacant at the time of our arrival.

Forty dollars was all the money I had when I landed at Lavaca. I therefore took in sewing and did all I could to support myself and daughter. All the money I got

[16] Frederick Law Olmsted, visiting Texas in 1853–54, wrote that Indianola had a "more busy and prosperous appearance" than Lavaca. At Lavaca, however, he heard of Indianola as "a little village down the bay." Schooners came to the wharves of Indianola and "with greater difficulty and with some liability to detention from grounding," to Lavaca. Frederick Law Olmstead, *Journey Through Texas*, (ed. by James Howard), 151–52.

for the half league of land was expended during the four years we lived at the town of M. House rent cost me as much as my living. I now had only to keep the house in repair I was in, and had no rent to pay. A month or two after we got settled, a young man came to seek board at our house and I took him. I found him polite and handy, as well as steady. He had no associates. He went to market for me every morning. He had not been many weeks with us when I saw he admired my daughter. I was not surprised at this, for my child was a lovely blossom of womanhood. Her soft, melting black eyes and long, silky black hair were universally admired. She was said to be not only pretty at this time but handsome, and was called a Belle. Her form was good. Tall and commanding in appearance, modest in demeanor, but lively in conversation. Many said she resembled me, but she was more like her father, especially in temper and disposition, for in this she was like me.

In a month or two I brought Mr. W[17] to an understanding. I told him my objections to him, without a home and only the clothes he stood in. He did not blame me, he said; it was natural as well as right I should be anxious for the welfare of my only child. He was acquainted with the history of her first marriage. After much remonstrating my daughter about the natural consequences of marrying a poor man, I saw her mind was made up to marry Mr. W. The day was set and they were married.

[17] John Watson.

Six months after my daughter married, the war between the North and South commenced, and as Mr. W had to go into the Southern army, he wished me to be with his wife until his return.[18] A lady in Lavaca wished me to take charge of her home, as she and her family were going to live in Victoria until the war was over. She had some colored servants and did not wish to be near the sea coast, fearing the enemy might come there.

I took charge of Mrs. E's property, and my daughter came to live with me. We got along during the war as best we could. Sometimes we had something to eat, and sometimes we were out of everything. Then came

[18] In a letter from Lavaca on May 7, 1862 (Manuscript Collection, Duke University Library), Ann indicated that John Watson "is a private in Chase Battalion at Salura Island. My daughter and self are now alone for the present. We are both well, and I am enjoying better health now than usual; hard times seems to agree with me." Ann Raney, whose spelling of proper names often depended on sound, probably meant Capt. D. D. Shea's battery, which served on the Texas coast. Harry McCorry Henderson, *Texas in the Confederacy*, 147. Major Shea, on December 28, 1862, from headquarters at Lavaca, ordered Captain S. T. Brackenridge, commander of the cavalry at Indianola, to destroy "the connections with the island," including the foot bridge over Ford Bayou, the bridge over Bobby Bayou, and the bridge over Powderhorn Bayou, and to dismantle the wharves. Special Order No. 25, signed by Major Shea, commanded Brackenridge to Saluria to secure "the services of Capt. Mainland and others who have interest in the place and who are desirous of driving their cattle off the island." Brackenridge was ordered to take a gallon of turpentine to "set every house on fire" and to take a keg of powder to "blow down the Light House at Pass Cavaloo." Albert O. Marshall, *Army Life: From a Soldier's Journal.*

the struggle when we did not receive our rations regularly as we ought to. The women would muster en masse, go to the men who were to deal them out to us, pistol in hands; and depend upon it, we got our rations, although previously refused. We walked back in triumph to our homes. Be assured that it was the women that protected themselves in this war and not the men. When out of firewood, we pulled down the first old building we came to, being instructed to do so by some men who were our friends, and often we had to battle for that.

One night a strong north wind was blowing and I heard a heavy crash close to our house. I got up and looked out and the Baptist church had blown down. I had been wishing for this some time, as it was a very old building. I ran to my daughter's room and told her to get up, and we both went to work to pack the lumber to the house before anyone was stirring. It was not yet day, but as soon as it came we found ourselves in possession of a lot of lumber for firewood. At daylight there were a dozen women packing it off to their homes, notwithstanding there was a little man placed over it to guard it and prevent anyone taking it off. He forbid us taking it, but all to no purpose. We told him there were enough of us to whip him, so he had as well say nothing. He was one of the citizens and we were well acquainted with him. He laughed at us for spunk. We threatened to tie him hand and foot if he should resist us.

One day we got out of meal, and many families were suffering for bread, so the first time we heard of them grinding meal for citizens, a good many ladies got together and went to ask for meal, but were refused, being told it was for citizens and not for us, and that we could not have any. A few ladies took charge of the man who refused us, and the rest went and filled up all the sacks, but not until we had threatened to set fire to the mill if we did not get it. One other time we went to press some rice of a merchant but instead of rice he sent us some meal.

The first of the war I made a good garden and planted about half an acre of corn, all of which I worked myself. Many times whilst at work I would be so hot and tired that I would cry like a child, for my daughter was in a situation that she could not help me. This garden was a great help to my family and I sold several dollars worth of vegetables.[19] I also raised one hundred chickens which was a great help in hard times.

The enemy was expected daily, and after having a skirmish on Chocolate Bayou,[20] they entered our town,

[19] In a letter to her niece, Ann asked about crops in North Carolina, saying, "They are very good in Texas. It has been very dry on the sea coast, but plenty of rain in the interior. Our warfs [*sic*] are full of cotton to go to Mexico and from there to England." Ann Raney Coleman to Alice Smith, May 7, 1862, Manuscript Collection, Duke University Library.

[20] Chocolate Bayou is the name of at least two Texas streams, probably named by the Spaniards who heard the term used by Indians and thought it referred to the color of the muddy water. The word used by Indians probably applied to the wild pepper indigenous to the coast and called *chiltipiquin*. Chocolate Bayou in northwestern Calhoun County empties into an inlet off Lavaca Bay. Webb, *The*

about fifteen hundred in all. They passed close to our house, within fifty yards. My daughter was much alarmed and it was with much persuading I got her to go to the window to look at them. They did not remain long in our town, but during their stay our town was set on fire. A strong north wind blowing at the time of the fire, it came very near destroying all the town, especially all the business portion was destroyed. I did not live immediately in town, yet we were close enough for the roof to catch fire. My daughter went upon the top of the house and I handed her water from the cistern and put it out, but we had to make haste and take everything out of the house into the prairie lest it might be burnt also. The wind abated about night and the fire in a measure subdued. Many people lost everything they possessed and caused much suffering. About eleven o'clock at night we moved all our things back to the house. I was so tired I threw a bed on the floor and went fast asleep, although the town was yet one sheet of flame. It was light enough to have picked up the smallest object.

I will not speak of a circumstance which happened to us while eating supper one evening whilst the Federal soldiers were in town. These soldiers entered our house by one door and three by another. They said to me, "Are there any of our men here?" "Who do you mean, sir?"

Handbook of Texas, I, 343. Frederick Law Olmstead wrote in his journal that "at a short causeway two or three miles from Lavaca we paid a heavy toll crossing the Chocolate, a small, crooked, dirty creek." Olmstead, *Journey Through Texas*, 150.

I replied. "Federal soldiers, Ma'am." "No, sir, there are not." "How do you get flour and coffee, Ma'am?" I replied, "We have a way to get it, sir." "We have been trying to starve you out for the last two years, but your supper table does not look much like it." "In this one thing," I said, "you will not find it so easy to do whilst there is a beef in our prairies."[21] "Are you a Union lady, Ma'am?" one of the men asked. "No, sir, I am surprised you should take me for one." "You do not seem to be afraid of us, made me think so." "That word afraid is not in my vocabulary, sir. I am one of the old Revolutioners of Texas." "Ah," he replied, "I thought you were something uncommon, you are so spunky." Asking me if I had any butter or eggs to sell and being told I had not, he departed with his comrades, a little wiser than when he came in about Texas women.

I will not say that our town was bombarded before I went to live at Mrs. E's house. I was staying with my

---

[21] In Special Order No. 25, signed by Major Shea, mention is made of the cattle located on the coast, and a Yankee soldier stationed on Matagorda Island commented that a large number of cattle "had at one time fed upon the island" and that

Matagorda Island seems to be the home of large droves of cattle. We saw a number of droves during our day's march. They were extremely wild. Every little while we would come near to a drove that were quietly grazing, or resting upon the rich grass. At our approach they would spring up and raise their shaggy heads, crowned with huge, unsightly horns of the Texas cattle, look upon us in wonder, and then gallop away in grand disorder for half a mile or so.

Marshall, *Army Life*, 315–16.

daughter in a house where behind the house was a battery of nine guns, and on this account we were obliged to leave the house during the time of bombardment, as it would not have been safe for us to have remained. We went one mile out of town and occupied another house, thinking ourselves protected from all danger here. One hour was given the citizens to leave the town. I was drinking a cup of coffee when the first shell came. We had determined upon going into a ditch close by whilst the bombardment was going on. My daughter had gone and her children with her, and a great many other ladies, but I stayed behind to drink my coffee, as this was the only stimulant I took, and I was determined not to be cheated out of that, as I could not well do without it. Whilst I was enjoying myself with this beverage there came a shell right over the house and landed in the garden about twenty yards from the house. I did not wait for a second one, but ran as quick as I could to the ditch, which was already full with about fifty ladies in it with their children.

On my reaching the ditch, I was requested by some of the ladies to put a piece of cotton in my ears, but this I declined to do, as I would rather hear all that was going on. A great many had their ears stopt full. The bombardment went on and the shells fell so close to us that our situation was a dangerous one. A Confederate officer rode up to the ditch and said, "Ladies, you must leave here immediately and go further up the coast. The enemy spies my men, the reserve, and are firing at them."

As they were hid in the bushes not ten steps from us, we flew, some one way and some another. I caught my daughter's little boy, Joseph Marks Henry by the hand, a child five years old, and my daughter with her baby only a few months old in her arms, and we ran as fast as our feet would carry us up the beach on the bay. I was crossing a bridge when one shell passed me within a yard or two. The wind from it was so strong that it was with difficulty I kept my feet. The little boy was thrown down by the force of the wind from the ball. We went two miles further up the coast, and as soon as the firing ceased at night, we returned home to cook some provisions for the next day.

Midnight saw us several miles up the coast. That night we were nearly smothered for want of air, they having fastened down the hatchway; and finding no one that knew how to open it until we were nearly all suffocated, some strong arm burst it open and we all jumped on the deck, one after another, as fast as we could. In the morning the firing commenced again. One of the Federal vessels being much injured, hauled off and left for good.[22] The other remained until night and left also. We again returned to our house and home.

[22] Lois Lucille Gray writes about the event in *Old Indianola*, 56–57:

Life moved in a natural sort of way until November 1, 1862, when three Yankee gunboats entered Pass Cavallo. Then Captain J. M. Reuss, with his company of Southern soldiers, fearing they would be cut off, since they were camped on Saluria Island,

Great excitement prevailed in town. Many families had not been heard from after the bombardment for several days, some having gone on the cars to Victoria. Mr. W, my son-in-law, was one of the battery men and could render his family no assistance at this time. When we were up the coast we had a good view of the bombarding. The two steamers fired eighty rounds of ball and shot before our batteries answered them, they being too far out in the bay to reach them; but on coming in closer, our batteries opened upon them in a praise worthy man-

---

and be without food, began to fire "Long Tom" and started retreating up the bay to Indianola.

Then the Yankee captain demanded the town to surrender. A loaded yawl was sent in under the flag of truce to take over the city. This was refused by Major Schea, the military commander. The best terms that could be obtained were two hours to move women, children and the sick. The yellow fever was raging at present, so those that were strong enough were moved. Others, too ill remained behind. . . .

In a thesis, "Indianola, Early Gateway to Texas" (73-75), written at St. Mary's University, Alice Freeman Fluth recorded:

There was a yellow fever epidemic at the time, and Major Schea was given an hour and a half to remove the sick women and children. When the time expired, the Federals started the bombardment of the town and continued the shelling until nightfall, having fired one hundred and seventy-five shells. The Confederates returned the fire, but at one, on the following day Indianola surrendered.

Federal troops did not occupy Indianola after it surrendered November 1, 1862, and during the spring and summer of 1863 some Confederate troops under Captain George were stationed at Indianola for eight months.

ner. The town was so densely covered with smoke and fire I thought once or twice it was on fire.[23]

[23] From Lavaca Ann wrote her niece:

. . . we have company at Victoria, who are at war amongst themselves, the Capt. of the company has to have 6 men to guard him all time to keep his own men from killing him. They cut down the major's tent to the ground the other night and were going to duck him, but he made his escape. There is petty subordination in camp. They object to both the major and Capt. as officers wishing to elect their own officers. They fell out with the Major because he objected to their stealing hogs and chickings They were displeased with their Capt. because he wants them to address him as Capt, and they call him Mr. Sutton.

Ann Raney Coleman to Alice Smith, May 7, 1862, Manuscript Collection, Duke University Library.

Sixth Book

In a few days after the bombardment, we moved back into town, to the house we had left, and a short time after this, we went and took charge of Mrs. E's property. There was at this time a nice garden of flowers, of which I am passionately fond, and I spent much time in it. I made a good garden and a crop of corn; the fodder brought me ten dollars. I had no assistance to work it, my daughter had not been in a situation to assist me; many times when at work the tears would come unbidden from my eyes; it was a kind of work I had not been used to, and too much for my years, but when I thought that my child and her children might suffer for bread, I worked with renewed strength.

The war being over, Mr. W returned to his family, and as there was no business at this time going on, every one at a loss to know what to do for a living and having a chance to take some Federal soldiers and officers to board, I did so; they amounted to seven officers and two privates. Servants were not to be had at this time, and I did all the work myself, my daughter's health not permitting her to help me but little. This was a pleasure to me to have it in my power to contribute to making a support for my daughter and children. As there was not work to be had, we were paid off in provisions, which were the same as money to us.

The day arrived for Mrs. E to return to her home, the Federal officers had all departed for their homes in the North, and Mr. W was obliged to get another house for his family. I had long wished to visit my niece, the only living child of my sister, who was residing with her father's brother in North Carolina. I had not seen her since she was three years old. I wished much to pay her a visit. I was without money and knew not how I should get means to go. I sold all the furniture I then possessed, books, pictures, and many relics of by-gone days, which with much reluctance, I parted from. . . .

This was in the year 1866; after bidding adieu to my child and husband, I was on the Gulf of Mexico, going to New Orleans. Nothing of much interest happened on my passage to Orleans except that a Negro woman was put in my charge, to take her ticket and see her on her way to Richmond, Virginia. I took her fare at New Orleans when I took my own. We stayed with my dear friends, Mr. and Mrs. F, who was very kind to us, and next day, early in the morning, her husband took us down to the depot and saw us off on the cars. At every station where we took in wood, the Negro woman went out of the cars to the nearest house and procured some boiling water, and having a small coffee pot along, I enjoyed a cup of this refreshing beverage very often. What coffee was left, I gave to my nearest neighbor. . . .

When I arrived, Mrs. Smith and her daughter, Eugina, and my niece came to meet me. I kissed them all, then went into the house. The sight of Alice, whose linements resembled those of her dear mother, caused tears to flow, and it was some time before I was composed enough to answer questions put to me by Mrs. Smith and her daughter. Alice, my niece, sat as one in a dream, scanning me from head to foot, for she no doubt had forgotten me since she had not seen me from three years old.

She was about sixteen years old, fair complexioned, large full blue eyes, and very light hair, inclined to be robust; her laugh was like silver bells for its sweet music. I did not take my eyes off her for several days. She was so much like her mother, for she was perfect symmetry in form. In a few months after my arrival in North Carolina, I got a village school to teach and went to work to enable me to lay up a little money to return home. I can say I liked the country much. The land is poor and cultivated with great labor. Cotton which I saw grows about one foot high; corn is also small, to Texas corn. Cattle is very small; fruit plentiful.

It was now the month of May, 1866, and after taking an affectionate leave of my niece and her friends, I left for Texas, that state that holds the bones of my dear parents and one brother—that state I love, for in her land I found friends; in her land I saw joy and sorrow, for here my parents breathed their last sigh; here I cheered the heart of our veteran soldiers as they went to battle for independence, who cried victory or death. They are men, true to duty, and her women lovely emblems of virtue and beauty, the vernal aspect of nature, the voluptuous foliage, terraced banks and Jesamine covered lattice, the balmy zephyrs and the Italian sky all tend to sublime. . . .

My child was looking for me and was glad I had arrived safe. I stayed with my daughter until January, '67. On the 15 of this month I went to teach Mrs. Spencer's children, they having six daughters all needing the advantages of an education. The house was in sight of my daughter's, which gave me the opportunity of seeing her every day or two, when the weather permitted. Mrs. Spencer's house being small, and very open the room I occupied, I took a bad cough and went to live with Mrs. Gorden Marten[1] until Mr. Spencer should build him a new building, which he contemplated to do and it was completed in one year from this time. . . .

Mrs. S was kind to me and after staying one year

[1] Ann Raney wrote her niece:

I am living with Mrs. Gorden Marten of Lavaca. I make my home with her at present. I was teaching awhile but am not at present time. My health is as good as I can expect at my time of life. I was 58 last November. Sis and family are well. We have plenty of rain, fruit will be plentiful this summer. Provisions are high. Flour best quality worth 14 dollars; second quality 10; sugar, 20 c; coffee, 25 pr. pound; bacon, 12 and 15 per pound; Gocian butter, 50 c specie.

Ibid., April 24, 1869, *ibid.*

with her I got a situation on the Lavaca River, to teach school to a private family for ten dollars per month, with privilege to take as many more as I could get. A few more came and I remained at this place one year. It was forty miles from Lavaca, where I was located; it was a beautiful location, situated on a hill surrounded by a forest of tall trees, a valley on both sides of the houses; the trees overshadowed the road both in the valley and on the elevated plain. . . .

I left for the town of L and stayed with my friend Mrs. M, my old friend, a month or so. My daughter's family, being now larger than before, nevertheless she was glad to see me, also her children. I made them several presents, which pleased them very much. I now was solicited to stay with Miss N. B,[2] who was keeping house for an uncle and wished my company until the arrival of her aunt, who she was daily expecting from New Orleans. Mr. and Mrs. W had no children, and they made Miss N. B their heir, and after Mr. W's death, which happened a short time after I left, Miss N. B went on to Philadelphia to get his property. . . .

Mrs. S,[3] a young married lady, wished me to go to

[2] On February 18, 1872, Ann wrote her niece, "I am staying at the present time with Miss Nora Barten and her uncle who has adopted Miss Nora as his heir." *Ibid.*, February 18, 1872, *ibid.*

[3] In letters, Ann refers to her as Mrs. Stanton, and it is possible that she was the Mrs. J. C. Stanton of Port Lavaca who on January 10, 1862, informed readers of the *Texas State Gazette* that the San Antonio House "is in good repair, and that she can accommodate her friends in the best manner. Good stables have been provided with careful hostlers."

the Island of Salura[4] to spend the summer. She was going
to stay with her father and wished me to accompany her.
She offered me a small compensation to go and assist her
with her household duties, so I concluded to go. . . . I had
the cooking to do as well as everything else to attend to—
the milk of fifteen cows to attend to, churning every day.
I also wrote three books for Mrs. S, my friend, putting
them together; and I, completing in manuscript form and
writing her also a copy.[5] . . . Clara wished me, when her
father broke up housekeeping, to go with her, but she had
no where but her sister's to go and I did not wish to be
chargeable to her friends, so we parted in the month of
October, 1872. . . .

They took me to the mouth of the Garcetes river,[6]

[4] Saluria is located on the northeastern bulge of Matagorda
Island and at the beginning of the Civil War was a thriving port and
ranching center. Webb, *The Handbook of Texas*, II, 537.

[5] Ann wrote much the same information in a letter on March
30, 1873, from Bolivar, Galveston:

> I have not had one letter from Mrs. Stanton since I left. She
> is indebted to me forty dollars, independent of the Book, which
> I wrote, for her, for publication. I wrote her three Books, and
> was to have half, as soon as she sold them. She is now living with
> her sister at Corpis Christa [*sic*]. Her sister is keeping a boarding
> house. I leave her in the hands of God, trusting that one day her
> conscience will haunt her. . . .

Ann Raney Coleman to "Dear Eugina," March 30, 1873, Manuscript
Collection, Duke University Library.

[6] Garcitas Creek, which rises in Victoria County, flows southeast and empties into Lavaca Bay. It is this stream which has been
identified as the one upon which Rene Robert Cavelier, Sieur de la
Salle, built Fort St. Louis, and which the Mexicans called the River of

where either not understanding the right channel or the boat drawing too much water, we could not affect an entrance, so we lay in the ball all night, it being too late to go to Lavaca. About midnight, as all slept but myself, I saw that the boat was fast filling with water. I therefore woke them up, and after getting a little over their scare, they both went to work in earnest, and it was well I found it out in time to save us all from going to the bottom. There was a hole knocked in the bottom of the boat. After bailing the water out all night, steadily, in the morning we pulled up anchor and were off for Lavaca. On landing myself and baggage, I went to the home of Mrs. Spencer, who received me kindly. I waited a few days before I found a conveyance to go to the Garcet, where my daughter was now residing with her family. . . .

It was a week or two after this I received a letter from Mrs. Baugh at Boliver Point[7] near Galveston wish-

---

the French. Garcitas, as applied by the Mexicans, means "the first horns of the deer" and is believed to have been used because of the similarity of the projections of the stream with those of the horns of a deer. Webb, *The Handbook of Texas*, I, 671.

[7] Bolivar Point is the southwestern tip of Bolivar Peninsula, which separates the eastern portion of Galveston Bay from the Gulf of Mexico. *Ibid.*, I, 183. From Bolivar, Galveston, Ann wrote her niece on March 30, 1872: "I am teaching a small school here. It is just such another out of the way place as Salura Island, immediately on the sea coast. We have to cross the bay, and Boliver channel, before we can get to Galveston. I am living with Mr. Baugh's family who are very kind to me and teaching school in their house." Ann Raney Coleman to Alice Smith, March 30, 1872, Manuscript Collection, Duke University Library.

ing me to come and teacher her children, offering me 75 dollars per year, and I accepted it. In a few more days after I had accepted of Mrs. Baugh's offer, I received another letter from a gentleman near Hallittsville,[8] making me a better offer as regards salary, but my word was given, and in a few more days I was off to Galveston on my way to Boliver Point. Mr. Baugh was farming. . . . Mr. Baugh got a gentleman who lived at Boliver Point to see me safe across the channel, and when I got across I found a carriage waiting to take me to Mr. B's residence. On my arrival, I met with a hearty welcome by all the family, and they gave me my choice to teach her children or take a school independent of her and her children. I chose to take a school, finding I could get fourteen paying scholars.

At the end of the first month I lost seven in one day, owing to a remark Miss B made. She told the scholars I was going to a picnic, and they were to go also, and that I intended to make all my scholars make a speech. Those that did not would have to take their books and go home. The fear of being sent home made them leave for good. This was a misfortune. Half my school was gone, and I knew no remedy. Mrs. Baugh and myself went to see their parents, and I told them I had no desire to make any one make a speech against their will, but all I could say had no effect to bring my scholars back. I now had no resource but endeavor to get a school somewhere else, so

[8] Hallettsville was founded in 1838, becoming the county seat of Lavaca County in 1852. *Texas Almanac*, 79.

after staying there three months, I left Mrs. B and went into another settlement, nine miles from Mrs. B, where I had 20 scholars.

I had a good school room and only for the board I had and the mosquitoes, which was so bad in the day time that we could not sit down without a smoke. After supper I went to bed that I might get under my bar and see a little peace. I would have been satisfied, but for this great annoyance. The first week I went into the Hamshire settlement,[9] as it is called, I thought it would be impossible for me to remain. I was eat up by these insects. You could not place a pin point on my body for scars and sores, which the mosquitoes had made. I soon found that my acquaintances in the neighborhood would be very limited, as society here was at a low ebb. . . .

1873 saw me a happier, though a poorer, woman than 1847. Could I but blot out this year of my life I think I could breathe more freely than I do. . . . I stayed there three months at this isolated place, a more desolate I never saw. In the month of September, I left. The worms had eat up the people's crops and they were no longer able to pay for their children's tuition. It was a season when flies are very bad, so I had to give five dollars to carry me nine miles to Mrs. Baugh's. . . .

I commenced my public school and continued it until December, when I could no longer get a place to teach in, so I was compelled to give it up. The school board allowed

[9] Hamshire, in western Jefferson County, Texas, is in an area settled in the 1830's. Webb, *The Handbook of Texas*, I, 763.

me fifty dollars, and I was to pay all expenses. The rent of my school room cost me ten dollars per month; board, ten dollars, so that I did not clear but thirty dollars, having made $100 during the year. Left Boliver with 90 dollars. I tried every way to get a room, but did not succeed, so on the 8 of January, 1874, I left for Galveston, being detained five days for reasonable weather to cross the channel.

I called upon all my friends before I left Galveston, who were sorry at my departure. I called upon the little Spanish woman[10] who was all the time abusing the English and bid her goodbye, also Mr. E, a friend of Doctor B, saw me and my baggage safe on board the steamer for Indianola, and I appreciated this kindness. On leaving the wharf, a band of musicians that was on board played us some good music. I was not sea sick but felt a little squeamish. Next morning we landed at Indianola, went to the Globe Hotel,[11] and ate breakfast and dinner, charging us six bits a meal. At one o'clock we left on the cars for Victoria. Whilst at Indianola I called upon an old friend who had known me for many years. She was very

[10] In the Journal, Ann noted that "the man and woman with whom I resided did not live agreeable together. She of Spanish birth. He English, and although I was there only six weeks they had a fight or two."

[11] Frederick Law Olmsted, visiting Texas, wrote of Indianola, "There is a 'Globe Hotel' in the city." Olmstead, *Journey Through Texas*, 156.

glad to see me and regaled me with coffee and peaches, and when I left, bid me write to her.

I arrived at Victoria about four o'clock in the evening and stayed all night at the Hall Hotel.[12] Next morning I hired a conveyance to take me to Mr. M on the Lavaca River, 28 miles from Victoria, having heard he wished a teacher. I had a colored man for my driver who knew nothing about the road, so we got lost several times before I got to my journey's end. I had to give a Mexican one dollar independent of my carriage hire to put us on the right road. After being lost some time we arrived at sun down at Mr. M's. I stayed all night with them and next morning I took the same carriage and went seven miles farther to see my daughter. She was at this time staying on the Navidad River. . . .

[I stayed with my daughter] from June till November, when I got a situation to teach a public school at Mossey Grove,[13] seven miles from Hallittsville. Salary 35 dollars per month. . . . My school was on Sunday a church, being built for this purpose; on Saturday, a Grangers' house; every other Sunday, a temperance house. I often found in the morning after a meeting of the Grangers the seats piled half a dozen high, which

[12] A. F. Hall kept the hostelry of the Hall Hotel open in Victoria until 1866, when he rented to W. J. Neely. J. S. Petty, Jr. (ed.), *A Republishing of the Book Most Often Known as Victor Rose's History of Victoria*, 60.

[13] Mossey Grove, also known as Mossey Springs, is located near Hallettsville. Webb, *The Handbook of Texas*, II, 242.

would have to be put in order before we could take up school.

This is the 19 day of February, 1876. Mrs. F,[14] a neighbor of my daughter, has come in her carriage to take me to stay with her a while, and I rejoice as it will give me a chance to get round. I have been as a bird in prison for ten months. . . . I do Mrs. F's house work and sewing and teach her little boy for my maintenance, and she has given me some clothing since I have been with her, and she is willing for me to stay with her until I can get a school. So by the help of God I hope to live and praise His name.

The horn blows at four in the morning for the working hands to get up. I arise every morning at this hour and make six beds and sweep and dust four rooms before breakfast. . . . Mrs. Farrow's daughter, who lived with her mother when I first came to live with Mrs. F, has gone to housekeeping for herself, so that Mrs. F and myself are now alone with the exception of an orphan girl, whose parents were Polanders. She is a good looking girl, with a good figure but very uncultivated manners and little or no education. My grandchild Joseph imagined himself in love with her. He is working for Mr. F.[15]

[14] Mrs. Lucinda Farrar. Ann Raney Coleman to Alice Smith, March 22, 1876, Manuscript Collection, Duke University Library. Other sources give the name as Mrs. Louisa Farrar.

[15] Ann wrote her niece that "Joseph is hired to Mr. Oliver Farrer to drive cattle, and work on the plantation when there is no stock to drive." *Ibid.*, May 3, 1876, *ibid.*

I remonstrated with him for placing his affections on an object so unworthy of him.

I had this girl under my tuition several months who would not learn anything, said she did not see the use of an education, and instead of learning her lessons would lay down on the floor in school hours and go to sleep. So Mrs. F took her away and let her pursue the house duties, for which she thinks she is better fitted than an education. My grandchild Joseph and myself have had several sharp words about this girl, who, as Byron says, born in the Garret, in the kitchen bred, from thence promoted to dress her Mrs. head.[16] But even this service she has not talent to do, dancing like a man and beating her feet upon the floor as hard as she can. This seems to be her chief amusement, cursing and swearing her highest accomplishment. I told Mrs. F that I would rather follow my grandchild Joseph Mark Henry to the grave than see him united in marriage to this girl. . . .

Mrs. F is a good hearted woman without education, can neither read or write, of Spanish birth, rich in cattle and worldly goods,[17] visited me when I was sick at my daughter's and sent me many nice things to eat, and guess-

[16] Ann was correct in citing her source: Byron's *A Selection.*

[17] To "My dear Alice," Ann wrote: "I have a good home where I am. Mrs. Farrar is well-to-do and has a splendid home. She is Spanish and a widow. One daughter, married, lives with her. She has three or four children. She is kind to me. It is likely that I will remain this summer with her as my health is not the best." Ann Raney Coleman to Alice Smith, March 22, 1876, Manuscript Collection, Duke University Library.

ing that I was not happy in my home took me to hers, where I have been ever since, with good diet and my own exertions to make my living. My health is much better. My cough troubles me but little, and although I receive no money for my labors, Mrs. F is very kind to me. She often makes me a present of a dress or pair of shoes and many other little articles. . . .

Mr. Oliver Farro[18] is the oldest son of Mrs. F, is gone most of his time taking care of his stock. He is energetic in business, philanthropy, a moralizer, a sage, quick in discernment and judicious, loves his wealth better than women, and told me he was afraid to enter the matrimonial bond lest he should get a woman that would not be congenial to him. Mr. Oliver Farro is good looking but not handsome, square made, black eyes and hair, and when he walks has an important air, not swagger.

[Joseph Mark Henry] is now about eighteen years of age and has a pride to go neatly dressed. I raised this boy until he was five years old and have ever been his friend as far as it was in my power, clothing him when I could find means to do so. He has never been chargeable to his parents for much clothing. He is now no better than an orphan. Mrs. Farrer gave him employment on her farm for a few months to drive stock, but unfortunately

[18] Oliver Farrer was described in a letter from Ann to her niece as ". . . single—who would marry if he could suit himself. He is rich. If you were here, I would try to recommend you to him. He is a fine young man." *Ibid.*, March 28, 1876, *ibid.*

[he] roped a cow one day which got away with the rope on her horns, and getting entangled in the woods, starved to death before she was found. For this offense he was turned away from Mrs. Farro's house, and there may be another cause—that Mrs. F would have had no objections to Joseph marrying the Polander girl Mary, but knowing my objections to her, she has had no further use for him, only as a passing stranger. . . . I just now saw Joseph. He is going to find some employment. He made me feel sorry to see him so shabbily dressed, riding on his horse without a saddle. My heart is made to feel for the wants of the poor. How much more when my own kin are in need. He looked sad himself.

. . . one morning Mrs. Farrer informed me that Oliver, her son, was going to be married and would want my room. Not a little surprised at this information, I replied, "Very well, Mrs. F, you shall have it." "Mr. Hayes,"[19] she said, "will be very glad to have you go and teach his children." "Yes," I replied, "he has been to see me several times but I would not leave you to go to them, but now I suppose I am at liberty to do as I please."

After giving notice to Mr. Hayes that I would be at his house in a few days, Mrs. Farrer took me in her carriage and went with me, and I bid adieu to my quiet home. Oliver had pushed the question of marriage very

[19] Among the earliest settlers on Garcitas Creek were J. V. Hayes, Rodolph Hayes, and Matt Hayes. Petty, *Victor Rose's History of Victoria*, 31.

close to myself and paid me much attention for several
months, but learning my determination never to marry
again and especially one younger than myself, he went
and made up with an old maid he had not been on speaking terms with for several months. . . . On entering my
duties at Mr. Hayes' I found two boys and a girl . . . so
delicate that they were absent half the time from their
school. In two months I had to give up teaching them, as
they could not bear confinement. . . . I thought I should
like a more retired home, so she [a "lady who moved in
first class society" in Victoria] took me to Mr. Christopher
Hill's in DeWitt County,[20] where I am now staying, a
place more congenial to my feelings and circumstances.

[20] Mr. and Mrs. Christopher T. Hill. Hill was listed by the
DeWitt County census of June 28, 1880, as a forty-two-year-old
farmer born in Alabama, the son of a father born in North Carolina
and of a mother born in Alabama. His wife Elen [*sic*] was twenty-six
years of age and a native of Texas. Her parents were born in Alabama.
The 1870 census lists C. T. and Ellen Hill as man and wife having
real estate valued at $6,000 and personal estate at $10,600. Chris T.
Hill, as he is listed in records of the Cameron Masonic Lodge No. 76,
Yorktown, DeWitt County, held membership from 1870 to 1875. He
transferred to the Acacia Lodge No. 434 and then to Cuero Lodge No.
409, remaining a member until 1881. Dixie Milton, assistant librarian,
Grand Lodge of Texas Library, Waco, Texas, to the editor, February
3, 1964.

Seventh Book

I hear occasionally from my lawyer, Mr. L. H. Plank[1] of Gonzales, who I have employed to attend to some property of my father's in England. As yet nothing has transpired to make my situation any better. No litigation has been instituted. He was employed in 1876. It is now '79 and he has wrote me that after a preliminary examination, which he has taken three years to accomplish, he sees no chance for me to recover one dollar of my father's estate and that he considers it a legal bankruptcy. I wrote him that he was of a different opinion to Lord Broughme, who was my father's counselor and gave it as his opinion that it was a bankruptcy of great fraud and illegality. I desired him to return me my papers and power of attorney. He wrote to send him two dollars to pay the postage, that the papers were in England. I wrote again to say as soon as I received the papers I would send him the money, but he

[1] Lewis H. Planck's professional card was printed in the July 28, 1877, edition of *The Gonzales Inquirer*, stating that his office was located one door north of Cox's building in Gonzales. A lawyer and land agent, he proposed to "buy and sell lands, investigate Titles and defend land claims in any part of the state."

has not sent them. Yet Mr. Hill wrote to him also to send me my papers, but he did not reply to Mr. Hill's letter. I suppose he intends for me to sue him for them. I still correspond with my cousin, Mrs. Thompson, in Glasgow, Scotland, and am sending them a transcript of my life, of which she is very proud. . . .

I rise at five in the morning, feed the chickens the first thing, set the table for breakfast, then make all the beds in the house, sweep the floors, dust the rooms. I then after breakfast teach a niece of Mr. Hill's[2] the solid branches of education. This being done, I then give Minne Hill a music lesson; by teaching her I instruct myself, as I have had no practice in music for years. Yet in my youth I was a good musician, having learned this branch of education seven years. For my services I get my board and washing. What spare time I have I read and sew. . . .

I will now endeavor to say one word in behalf of my friend Mr. H. This winter he lost one thousand head of sheep from the severity of the winter, besides twenty thousand dollars of his wife's fortune, which has reduced him so much in money fund that he has had to live harder than he ever did before. When I first came to live with them, they set a good table and did not lack for any thing comfortable, but now he lives like a very poor man. Nothing but bread and meat and coffee without sugar.

[2] Minnie Hill was the niece of Mr. and Mrs. Christopher T. Hill. The 1880 census states that she was twelve years of age, a native of Texas. Her mother was a Texan and her father a native of Alabama. This census also indicates that Minnie was attending school.

When strangers come to the house to eat, a little better is set on the table. On this account I do not ask Mr. H for one dollar. . . .

Mr. Plank has at last sent my papers to Mr. Hill, all but a letter from Couts and Co. Bankers, a very important letter, also a letter from my sister to myself. I will get Mr. Hill to write to him for them. Mr. Hill is a Mason and Mr. Plank is one. That is why I got my papers from Mr. Plank, or I might have had to sue for them. He had wrote and scribbled upon one of my deeds, defacing it much—a very ungentlemanly act, say the least of it.

It is the last of September. The birds begin slowly to expand their close winter folds. The woods, though still green, show an imperceptible yellow and purple tint; nests of variegated flowers adorn the green sward, nameless, yet deserving a name for their beauty. Everything portrays an Eden on earth, yet many are not satisfied with their situation. Mr. H speaks determinedly of selling his place and going to the mountains amongst Indians for to make his home.

One evening as I sat in conversation with Mrs. Hill, a gentleman in his carriage rode up to the gate. It was Mr. Nicholes,[3] who lived a few miles from Mr. Hill's. He

[3] Possibly Lazarus Nichols. On the same page of the 1870 DeWitt County census that lists C. T. Hill is information about Lazarus Nichols, forty-two, a farmer and stockraiser. Born in Missis-

said he had come to get me to teach school for him. He wanted a public school. I did not want to teach a public school as I was afraid I would not pass my examination in some branches that would be required of me, for my memory was failing me every year. Mr. Nicholes then said, "If you do not pass your examination, I will pay you to teach my own children at home." I then consented to go to his home and left Mr. and Mrs. Hill, not without regret.

A week after I left Mr. Hill's house I went to Cuero and stood my examination and passed in every study and branch except arithmetic. I was deficient in fractions only, but the professor, Mr. Nash,[4] said I was competent to teach any private school and if it had been left to himself, he would have passed me to teach a public school but that he was under oath to the district judge,[5] to pass no one who

sippi, he was married to a native of Texas and was the father of six children, ranging in ages from one to nineteen years.

[4] David W. Nash operated Guadalupe Academy in Cuero from 1873 to 1910. Webb, *The Handbook of Texas*, I, 442. In the census of DeWitt County for 1880, a school teacher named D. Nash was listed as living on Esplanade Street, Cuero. Born in Virginia of native Virginian parents, he was thirty-nine years of age. *The Cuero Record* of December 31, 1935, indicates that D. W. Nash opened his school in 1873, and when it developed into Guadalupe Academy he served as principal. The school "for years remained the leading institution in the Southwest."

[5] Miss Waurine Walker, assistant director of the Division of Teacher Education and Certification of the Texas Education Agency, in a letter to the editor (February 28, 1964), wrote: "The laws enacted during this period did not specifically specify that the Board of Examiners or persons appointed to administer teacher's examinations were under oath to the district judge. In most instances they were

was not perfect in arithmetic.[6] After I returned home, Mr. Nicholes told me to go on and teach his children with some four or five others in the neighborhood, which instructions I followed over three months.

. . . when Mr. Ball, an Englishman[7] by birth, came to the house, I asked him if his lady would not like to have me to assist her in her household affairs, as I wished to leave Mr. N's family. He said his wife would like to have me for company as he was often gone from home, and that I could assist her in her household affairs. He set a day to come after me.

Mr. Ball understood music and often played on the piano. He was a good singer. He had been acquainted with

───────

appointed by the district judge since this was required by law and the individuals on the Board of Examiners were responsible to the judge."

[6] In *ibid*. Miss Walker states:

The law did not make any specific reference to the fact that a perfect score on a subject had to be achieved before the individual was qualified to teach in the public schools. . . . the person who took the examination was expected to have an average grade of not less than 75 per cent and a grade of not less than 50 per cent on each subject. We do not find any reference in the law to the fact that an individual had to make a perfect score. It could be that a county judge or a county Board of Examiners might at the time of the 1880 examination had insisted upon such a score but there is no reference in the school laws to such a specific requirement.

[7] A Thomas Ball, thirty-one, is listed in the 1880 census of DeWitt County, Texas. He named farming as his occupation and England as his birthplace. His wife, Mary, twenty-eight, was a native Texan.

Mr. N's family some time. I got acquainted with Mr. B at Mr. Hill's. He set a day to come after me and I prepared to leave. I had spent four months as unpleasantly as I could spend it. . . . I had been three months at Mr. Ball's when he sold out everything he had except a flock of sheep, homestead, cattle, horses, hogs; and his wife, Mrs. B, went to her father's with her two children. Mrs. B did not like a country life. She had been raised in the city of Victoria and her heart yearned for to go to her city home. Mr. B was on the prairie with his sheep, camping out of a night with his sheep. I was comfortable enough as regards a room, but they had nothing for me to do but nurse a seven-months baby from morning to night, which was too much for my strength, as he was a very heavy child.

This is the spring of 1881. Our winter was severe and cold. Mr. Nockey[8] lost 600 head of sheep, a great loss to him as he is only in moderate circumstances. His wife quite a sickly woman, half her time unable to attend to her household duties. His means limited, he informed me this morning that he would not be able to keep me to teach his children another month, but he said, "Mrs. T, you can have a home with my family as long as you want." I thanked him and told him the next time he went to town, I would like to go with him as I would try to get a

[8] Ferdinand Noelke, thirty-seven, a farmer, and his wife, Alice, thirty-three, were included in the census of DeWitt County, Texas, taken July 10, 1880. Their children, four sons, all native Texans, included Montgomery, seven; Willie, six; Emmett, four; and Johnny, three. Noelke was born in Prussia and his wife in New Jersey.

school in Cuero. I told him I sympathized with him in the loss of his sheep.

I am this November 74 years of age. After staying a few months with my daughter, I went to stay with Mrs. Farrer, an old friend of mine on the Garcetas River. She was glad to see me at her home once more. I taught her grandchildren, a boy and girl, for three months and then the public school opened and she sent them to it. I again returned to my daughter's. And the last of July, 1886, I went to live with Mrs. George Willey in Victoria and I do a little sewing for my board and washing, and she is kind as a sister to me. This is 1887. I have been with her eight months and am 76 years old and hope to make my home with her as long as God is willing.

Mr. Willey has to move to Cuero and I am going with them. After being in Cuero one year Mr. Willey took sick and was three months that he was not able to do any work and he came near dying. They had to go in debt for provisions and clothing. They were not able to take care of me, and although they did not tell me so and would have divided their last piece of bread with me, I felt it a duty to get some other house. But until I went to see the County Commissioners, I could not move anywhere, so I went and met them and they allowed me eight dollars a month.[9] There was another reason I wished to

---

[9] "I now get my support off the County," Ann wrote her niece. "It is only eight dollars a month. I am staing with a lady who keeps Private boarding house or she could not afford to take me for eight

move. She had three grown boys who sat up late at night and made so much noise I could not sleep, so to get rid of them I had to leave, for which I was sorry.[10] I had been two years and six months in their family, and they were kind to me.

I found a lady who kept a boarding house, Mrs. S, who knew me for years and had always been kind to me. She boarded me for eight dollars. She could not have afforded to do it if she had not had other boarders. Mr. Willey was like his lady—kind hearted. He was an engineer on the train. They had seven children, five boys and two daughters. I have petitioned the legislature[11] for

dollars a month." Ann Raney Coleman to Alice Smith, November 29, 1888, Manuscript Collection, Duke University Library.

[10] Late in November, Ann wrote that she had "been busey moveing my things to Mrs. Swifts, as I could no longer stand the way Mrs. Willy let her children treat me." *Ibid*. The following month she explained to "my dear and much beloved neice," that "Mrs. Willy began to get tired of me and she allowed her children to spit in my face and curse and abuse me so I moved on the childrens account." In this letter she indicated that Mrs. Swift was a widow. *Ibid.*, December 22, 1888, *ibid*.

[11] In March, 1882, Ann was requesting information from state officials, writing from Cuero to James B. Goff, an attorney, indicating that she had corresponded with Judge M. L. Hunter, one of the members of the Board of Veterans. "I am teaching a small school in Cuero and often feel incapacitated for doing it and need more care than I can take of my self I find it very difficult with all of my exertions to get along." Ann Raney Coleman to James B. Goff, March 31, 1882, University of Texas Archives.

Goff wrote Governor Oran M. Roberts, stating Ann's case:

I have investigated her case out of sympathy for unfortunate condition and have been satisfied from what I have learned, that

a pension, but they would not grant me one on account of my marrying twice. This is an unjust law. The man can marry as many times as he wants to, and they allow him his pension. But woman, the weaker vessel, if she marries again is deprived of a living the balance of her days.

I have been 34 years a widow from my last husband and lost every vestige of my property in the '36 war and only saved the clothes I stood in and a few papers of my father's and mother's and am now homeless and destitute. Too old to make my living, yet I am cast off by the legislature as a branch to be withered or as a tree driven by the lightning's blast. Oh, what a stain on the national escutcheon of Texas! Performed services when a girl

---

her statements are true and that she is as deserving if not more so of some bounty from the state as many who have received Veteran Certificates.

She is very old, bears an excellent character and is very needy; and if you can conscientiously recommend the Legislature to aid her by a donation of a small piece of the public domain which the Railroads hav'nt gobbled up, I think it will be well-timed charity.

James B. Goff to Governor Oran M. Roberts, April 12, 1883, *ibid*. To Governor Roberts, on July 25, 1880, while residing with Mrs. E. L. Blackwell in Cuero, Ann mentioned, " . . . I have laid several letters before Commissioners, at Austin Stateing my circumstances, one was taken by Mr. George Finley another by Mr Crain which failed to meet with aney responce, during those times Mr. Bryant was secretary to the Veteran association, he is a great friend of Mr. Robert Mills formerly Banker at Galveston and I have good reason to think that Mr Bryant, was impressed by Mr R Mills to do nothing in my favor. . . ." Ann Raney Coleman to Governor Oran M. Roberts, July 25, 1880, Asbury Papers, University of Texas Archives.

before my marriage which serves recognition of our government, but because the men are dead who know I performed these services, I must go without reward. I took ammunition on horseback 15 miles half way to Velasco for the Battle of Velasco and placed it in the hollow of a tree for Captain Brown to go after or send for it, and on my return home I was followed by two Mexican spies and it was a race for life. Had I not had the best horse they would have caught me.[12] I was proud to perform the act and would not have mentioned it as expecting any pay for it had I not been treated so harshly by our legislature.

My daughter is very low with an incurable disease called cancer. They sent for me a week ago to go and see her. They sent me money or I could not have gone. I found her very low and after staying one week, returned to Cuero, my present home, as my daughter was some better. Before I left the doctor told me she was liable to die any moment, so I do not know what moment they will send after me again. I am very sad and broken down in spirits at the thought of losing my only child.

[12] In writing Governor Roberts, Ann said: "At the Battel of Velasco I moulded bullets and made the patches and took them on my horse 15 miles, to Mr Bertrands ranch for our men to come after them. I was persued by two spies, but had the best horse, and made my escape." *Ibid*.

Post Journal

Victoria Thomas Watson died in Cuero on August 10, 1890, and her mother was taken ill the same day, remaining under a physician's care for three weeks.[1] By September 7, 1890, she had recovered sufficiently to write her niece, ". . . we have had two months of dry weather. We were out of drinking water but we have had a little rain for two or three days which has give us some water. We had one or two cases of small pox in town. Scared every one but there is none now. They have had it bad in Mexico and maney other places. . . ."[2]

A note edged in black and signed Addie Saldana, Cuero, was sent to "my dear Cousin," March 25, 1891, explaining that "our grandma is not so well. She has a very bad cold and has not been so well, poor old lady. She is failing in health every day. She will not live long I am afraid."

Addie's prediction did not materialize, for Ann Cole-

[1] Ann Raney Coleman to Alice Smith, October 15, 1890, Manuscript Collection, Duke University Library.
[2] *Ibid.*, September 7, 1890, *ibid.*

man wrote from Cuero on October 1, 1891, that finances concerned her. She observed that she had to ". . . pay one dollar for my washing and one dollar shoues and cloathing which makes 36 dollars more than the county gives me."[3]

After writing her niece, Ann made another move:

. . . Mrs. Swift has moved to her other house which she owns, and did not have enough room for me and her Clerks in the store. I am boarding now [with] Mrs. Brown, a widow Lady at the Gulf Hotel. She takes me for the same amount as Mrs. Swift, 9 dollars a month. I have better Board and she gives me a room to my self, but how long she will let me stay I do not know as hotels are often crowded and she might need her Room. She is a member of my church.[4]

Ann Raney Coleman died in Cuero in March, 1897.

[3] *Ibid.*, October 1, 1891, *ibid.*

[4] The *Cuero Weekly Star* of March 6, 1874, contains an advertisement for the Gulf Hotel. Owned at that time by D. and W. S. Brown, the hotel was advertised as "a new and complete building in every respect. Rooms comfortable and well ventilated. Table supplied with the very best the market affords."

Bibliography

I. UNPUBLISHED MATERIALS

A. *Manuscript Collections*

Asbury Papers, Texas State Library Archives.

Dr. Samuel E. Asbury to Miss Harriet Smither, October 2, 1945.

Dr. Samuel E. Asbury to Miss Harriet Smither, January 16, 1946.

Asbury Papers, University of Texas Archives.

Ann Coleman to Governor Oran M. Roberts, July 25, 1880.

Bascom Giles, commissioner of the General Land Office of the State of Texas, to Dr. Samuel E. Asbury, May 5, 1944.

Nannie M. Tilley to Dr. Samuel E. Asbury, June 22, 1944.

Claims Correspondence, Texas State Archives.

Ann Coleman, New Orleans, to the comptroller of Texas, August 1, 1852.

Comptroller of Texas to Ann Coleman, September 1, 1852.

Collection of Mrs. L. G. Rich, Stephenville, Texas.

Dr. Samuel E. Asbury to Mrs. E. L. Lehman, Angleton, Texas, July 3, 1947.

John H. Herndon land transfer to David G. Mills (penciled note).

Map of Velasco, Texas, area showing plantation of Peter Gabriel Bertrand.

Mills and Mills v. *Thomas*, with attachment order attached, Second Judicial District of the Republic of Texas court record, Judge Benjamin C. Franklin, March 4, 1837.

Moses S. Patton land transfer to Edwin Waller, February 24, 1837.

Manuscript Collection, Duke University Library.

Addie Saldana to Alice Smith, March 25, 1891.

Ann Raney Coleman to Alice Smith, May 7, 1862; April 24, 1869; February 18, 1872; March 30, 1872; March 22, 1876; March 28, 1876; May 3, 1876; September 24, 1877; May 1, 1886; November 29, 1888; December 22, 1888; September 7, 1890; October 15, 1890; October 1, 1891.

Ann Raney Coleman to "Dear Eugina," March 30, 1873.

J. Locke Smith to "Dear Clinton," January 29, 1853.

J. Locke Smith to W. B. Smith, Spring Grove, N.C., May 3, 1849.

University of Texas Archives.

Ann Raney Coleman to James B. Goff, March 31, 1882.

James B. Goff, Austin, Texas, to Governor Oran M. Roberts, April 12, 1883.

B. *Single Letters to the Editor*

Dixie Milton, assistant librarian, Grand Lodge of Texas Library, Waco, Texas, February 3, 1964.

Mrs. L. G. Rich, Stephenville, Texas, December 8, 1963.

Waurine Walker, assistant director, Division of Teacher Education and Certification, Texas Education Agency, February 28, 1964.

C. *Theses*

Boozer, Jessie Beryl. "The History of Indianola, Texas." Master's thesis, The University of Texas, 1942.

Bridges, J. L. "The History of Fort Bend County." Master's thesis, The University of Texas, 1939.

Covington, Mrs. Sidney C. "The 'Runaway Scrape': An Episode of the Texas Revolution." Master's thesis, The University of Texas, June, 1942.

Fluth, Alice Freeman. "Indianola, Early Gateway to Texas." Master's thesis, St. Mary's University, 1939.

Marrs, John Columbus. "The History of Matagorda County." Master's thesis, The University of Texas, August, 1928.

II. PUBLIC RECORDS

A. *United States Government Records*

Fifth Census of the United States (1830), Louisiana.

Sixth Census of the United States (1840), Louisiana.

Seventh Census of the United States (1850), Louisiana.

Ninth Census of the United States (1870), DeWitt County, Texas.

Tenth Census of the United States (1880), DeWitt County, Texas.

B. *State Records*

Census of Austin's Colony, 1826.

C. *County Records*

Marriage bond, John Thomas and Ann Rainey (*sic*), Brazoria County, Texas, February 14, 1833.

Marriage bond, Samuel Hoit and Mary Raney, Brazoria County, Texas, April 22, 1834.

Marriage license, Alexander Perro and Alice A. Watson, DeWitt County, Texas, June 19, 1882.

Marriage license, Jean Thevinet and Ann M. Watson, DeWitt County, Texas, June 19, 1882.

III. NEWSPAPERS

Brazoria Advocate, 1834.

Constitutional Advocate and Texas Public Advertiser (Brazoria, Texas), 1833.

Cuero Daily Star, 1873, 1874.

Cuero Record, 1935.

Cuero Weekly Star, 1874.

Daily Picayune (New Orleans), 1953, 1954.

Dallas Morning News, 1886.

Gonzales Inquirer, 1877.

New-Orleans Bee, 1832.

New York Daily Times, 1853.

Standard (Clarksville, Texas), 1872.

Telegraph and Texas Register (Brazoria, Texas), 1836, 1837, 1842.

Texas State Gazette (Port Lavaca, Texas), 1862.

Times (London), 1830, 1854.

Victoria Advocate, 1876.

IV. BOOKS

Barker, Eugene. *Annual Report of the American Historical Association for the Year 1922.* 2 vols. Washington, D.C., United States Government Printing Office, 1928.

Biographical and Historical Memoirs of Louisiana. Chicago, The Goodspeed Publishing Co., 1892.

Blake, Vernon. *Goliad.* Goliad, Texas, Goliad Publishing Co., 1938.

Brown, John Henry. *History of Texas.* 2 vols. St. Louis, L. E. Daniell, Publisher, 1862.

————. *The Life of Henry Smith.* Dallas, A. D. Aldridge Co., 1887.

Clement, William Edwards. *Plantation Life on the Mississippi.* New Orleans, Pelican Publishing Company, 1952.

Collier's Encyclopedia. New York, Crowell-Collier Press, 1963.

Coues, Elliott, ed. *Forty Years a Fur Trader on the Upper Missouri, the Personal Narrative of Charles Larpenteur, 1833–1872.* New York, E. P. Harper's, 1898.

Davis, Edwin Adams. *Plantation Life in the Florida Parishes of Louisiana, 1836–1846, As Reflected in the Diary of Bennet H. Barrow.* New York, Columbia University Press, 1943.

Fortier, Alcee. *Louisiana*. 2 vols. Madison, Wis., Century Historical Association, 1914.

Fossler, Albert E. *New Orleans, The Glamour Period*. New York, The Pelican Publishing Co., 1957.

Friedrichs, Irene Hohmann. *History of Goliad*. Victoria, Texas, Regal Printers, 1961.

Gray, Lois Lucille. *Old Indianola*. San Antonio, The Naylor Company, 1950.

Heller, John H. *Galveston City Directory, 1872*. Galveston, Texas, The Galveston News, 1872.

Henderson, Harry McCorry. *Texas in the Confederacy*. San Antonio, The Naylor Company, 1955.

Hill, Jim Dan. *The Texas Navy*. New York, A. S. Barnes, 1962.

Hollon, W. Eugene, and Ruth Lapham Butler, eds. *William Bollaert's Texas*. Norman, University of Oklahoma Press, 1956.

Kendall, John Smith. *History of New Orleans*. 2 vols. New York, The Lewis Publishing Co., 1922.

King, Dick. *Ghost Towns of Texas*. San Antonio, The Naylor Company, 1953.

Marshall, Albert O. *Army Life: From a Soldier's Journal*. Joliet, Ill., printed by the author, 1884.

Morris, Homer F., J. R. Baxter, Jr., Virgil O. Stamps, and W. W. Combs, comps. *Favorite Songs and Hymns*. Dallas, Stamps-Baxter Music & Printing Co., 1939.

Muir, Andrew Forest, ed. *Texas in 1837*. Austin, University of Texas Press, 1958.

Olmstead, Frederick Law. *Journey Through Texas*. Ed. by

James Howard. Austin, Von Boeckmann-Jones Press, 1962.

Partridge, Eric. *A Dictionary of Slang and Unconventional English*. New York, The Macmillan Company, 1938.

Petty, J. W., Jr., ed. *A Republishing of the Book Most Often Known as Victor Rose's History of Victoria*. Victoria, Texas, Book Mart, 1961.

Quennell, Peter, ed. *Byron, a Self Portrait*. London, John Murray, 1950.

Robinson, Duncan W. *Texas 3-Legged Willie*. Austin, Texas State Historical Association, 1948.

Schiwetz, Buck. *Buck Schiwetz' Texas*. Austin, University of Texas Press, 1960.

Seltzer, Leon E., ed. *The Columbia Lippincott Gazetteer of the World*. Morningside Heights, N.Y., Columbia University Press, 1952.

Sinclair, Harold. *The Port of New Orleans*. Garden City, N.Y., Doubleday, Doran & Company, Inc., 1942.

Smithwick, Noah. *Evolution of a State*. Austin, The Steck Company, 1935.

Smith, Travis L., ed. *A History of Brazoria County, Texas*. (No place), 1958.

Strobel, Abner. *Old Plantations and Their Owners of Brazoria County, Texas*. Houston, The Union National Bank, 1930.

Tallant, Robert. *The Romantic New Orleanians*. New York, E. P. Dutton and Co., 1950.

Texas Almanac. Dallas, A. H. Belo Corporation, 1953.

Visit to Texas, Being the Journal of a Traveller. Austin, The Steck Company, 1952.

Webb, Walter Prescott, ed. *The Handbook of Texas.* 2 vols. Austin, The Texas State Historical Association, 1952.

Wilcox, Cadmus M. *History of the Mexican War.* Washington, D.C., The Church News Publishing Company, 1892.

Williams, Charles Richard. *The Life of Rutherford Birchard Hayes, Nineteenth President of the United States.* 2 vols. Boston, 1914.

Winters, John D. *The Civil War in Louisiana.* Baton Rouge, Louisiana State University Press, 1963.

Work Projects Administration Writers' Program. *Louisiana, A Guide to the State.* New York, Hastings House Publishers, 1947.

Yoakum, Henderson. *History of Texas From Its First Settlement in 1685 to Its Annexation to the United States in 1846.* Austin, The Steck Company, 1935.

V. ARTICLES

Brindley, Anne A. "Jane Long," *The Southwestern Historical Quarterly,* Vol. LVI (October, 1962), 2, 237.

Garrett, Kim S. "Family Stories and Sayings," *Singers and Storytellers,* Texas Folklore Society Publications, Vol. XXX (1961), 277.

Kennedy, Martin M. "The Wild Woman of the Navidad," *Legends of Texas,* Texas Folklore Society Publications, Vol. III (1924), 242–53.

Kilman, Ed. "Heartbeats in Old Brazoria," *Houston Post*, September 10, 1944.

Nixon, Pat Ireland. "Dr. Benjamin Harrison, Temporary Texans," *Journal of the History of Medicine and Allied Science*, Vol. 1, No. 1, 110–11.

Swanson, Gloria. "Bailey's Light," *Backwoods to Border*, Texas Folklore Society Publications, Vol. XIX (1943), 144–45.

White, Alice Pemble. "The Plantation Experience of Joseph and Lavinia Erwin, 1807–1836," *The Louisiana Historical Quarterly*, Vol. 27, No. 2 (April, 1944), 407.

Index

cough, 120; teaches school, 150ff.; during Civil War, 153–55; garden of, 155; returns from United States, 164–65; teaches at Mrs. Spencer's, 165; lives with Baughs, 169; lives with Farrars, 163ff.; teaches music at Mr. Hill's, 179ff.; takes teacher's examination, 181; teaches at Lazarus Nichols', 181; moves to Thomas Ball's, 183; moves to Victoria, 184; moves to Cuero, 184; pension of, 184, 185 & n.; services in the Texas Revolution, 187; lives with Mrs. Brown, 189; death of, 189

Coleman, John: 122 & n.; marries Ann Raney, *xiv*, 124; sued for divorce by Ann Raney, *xv*, 149; described, 124; mistreatment of Ann Raney, 132, 148–49; vision, 133; leaves, 139; returns, 147–48

Colorado River: 125

Comanche (ship): 19n.

Conner, Mr. (Colemans' boarder): 117

Convention of 1824: 27n.

Convention of 1832: 21n.

Cotton, Mr. (second mate on *St. George*): 6ff.; proposes to Ann Raney, 7

Counsel, Dr. Jesse: 41, 43, 44–46, 52, 71

Counsel, Mrs. Jesse: 41, 44–47ff.

Couts & Co., Bankers: 180

Crain, William H.: 186n.

Cuba: 7, 13

Cuero, Tex.: 181ff.

Cumberland, England: *x*

Cutware, Mrs. (boarded Mrs. Coleman): 109

D., Judge: 73

Dallas, Tex., Opera House: *viii*

Daphney (Negro cook): 72

DeWitt County, Tex.: 177

Dickinson, Charles Henry: *xiii*, 107 & n.

Donaldsonville, La.: *xiii*, 96 & n., 100

Dress: 14; wedding trousseau, 55

E., Mrs. (Mrs. Coleman in home of): 153, 162–63

E., Mr.: 171

East Prairie, Tex.: *x*n.

Eliza (Negro girl): 102

Emerton (ship): 12

Entertainment: 27, 44–45

Erwin, Isaac: 101n.

Erwin, Joseph: *xiii*

F., Mrs. (Mrs. Coleman's friend): 139ff.

Fannin, J. W.: *xii*, 79n.

Fanny Butler (ship): 19n.

Farrar, Mrs. Lucinda: 173ff., 184

Farrar, Oliver: 173n., 175

Ferryboats: 88

Finley, George: 186n.

Franklin, Benjamin C.: 93n., 98n.

Fredonian Rebellion: 61n.

Fryer, Maj.: 142n.